A Man's Foes, Volume 2

A MAN'S FOES.

BY

E. H. STRAIN.

'A man's foes shall be they of his own household.'

VOL. II.

SECOND EDITION.

LONDON:
WARD, LOCK & BOWDEN, LIMITED
WARWICK HOUSE, SALISBURY SQUARE, E.C.
NEW YORK AND MELBOURNE.
1895.

LOAN STACK

CONTENTS OF VOL. II.

415

CONTENTS

A MAN'S FOES

CHAPTER XIV.

HOW A PARTY RID OUT OF CLONCALLY AND RID STRAIGHT BACK AGAIN.

SURE and indeed, carefulness beset our pillows at our wakening, as how could it miss when danger threatened us on every side? That which was the nearest was doubtless the presence of the two score men that lay in the barn; it was like to be no easy matter to be clean rid of them. For themselves, we were more than a match for them, there being now fifteen men within the house, or better than one to three— ours well armed and skilful of their weapons; they provided with but poor makeshifts, and little disciplined even in the use of these. But, then, they had a regiment at their back. It were a pretty pickle should they bring the whole hive of bees about our ears.

Captain Hamilton's first waking words were of this very thing.

'Upon my word, Mary,' said he, 'I could go nigh to wishing that your charity had been with my peace of mind last night, and that was far enough to seek. It begins to have a plaguey look of blundering, this of showing the thieves the road to the larder.'

It had, and not a word had I to say to the contrary. But afterwards, when the same matter came up in talk at the table, there was no lack of champions, each of my guests vying with the rest in finding good reason and sufficient for all that I had done.

'Why, man!' Mr. Browning exclaimed—to be sure, he had been mine abettor before the fact—'why, Hamilton! what would you have? The choosing was no better than between two evils. One would think you knew not the boldness of an empty stomach. Faith! I do; and I was glad enough to hear of meat to pacify the mob that was at the door last night between five and six of the clock.'

Mr. Canning had likewise his word to say.

'Sure, Hamilton, it's neither you nor I that should find fault,' said he; 'for had they been wandering at large all about your policies, it strikes me we'd have had some difficulty in getting into the house at all, let alone unobserved, as we did. It's *ill quarrelling with the horse that sets you across the river*, as the saying hath it.'

'I'm none so sure of that,' said Captain Hamilton, 'if the beast shows an inclination to buck you off in the middle. I'm not finding fault, my dear friends—far from it, I assure you ; but if my wife herself will deny that it hath more the marks of a woman's pity than of a man's judgment, she's not the woman I take her for !'

'And so it was, past all controversy, more credit to her!' exclaimed Mr. Browning. 'But that it averted a great danger is every whit as evident.'

'Like enough indeed,' said my husband, 'for the moment. The difficulty now is to be rid of them entirely, and that's like to be a pretty tough riddle, I'm afraid. If any of you hath a glimpse of the answer, I'll be thankful to him to declare it; for my part, I'm lost in the deepest darkness.'

'I see little mystery,' said Mr. Browning, 'in facing them with the plain truth—to wit, that having cleared the larder here for their supper, they must go further afield to find their breakfast. And I'd have as little hesitancy in ordering them off the premises, or in kicking them off, if they loiter. What say you, Mr. Canning ?'

'What! would you take up arms against the King's men?' asked my husband. 'There might be awkward consequences to follow that, Browning, as I know to my cost.'

'Not arms, but legs!' said Mr. Browning. 'And that reminds me that you'll have to suffer me to try it, at any rate; you can't go within sight of them, Hamilton, proclaimed as you are——'

'Oh, but won't I, though!' broke in my husband; 'faith, it's see the men that have ousted Mountjoy's I'll do, and that before the sun's an hour higher. A set of idle good-for-naughts! not one of them stirring yet, I believe, and eight of the clock gone ten minutes ago.'

But at this we all fell to expostulating with one accord; for every word he could say in favour of his intention, we had ten, and more, to say against it. Indeed, it was flat madness for a man that had a price on his head to show himself to a King's regiment; and to do it without the least necessity in the world were no longer madness merely, but crime. So Mr. Canning and Mr. Browning told him roundly; we women bringing persuasion to bear, while they tried the power of a rating. At last, not finding a word to say in answer to what we had to urge, he could not choose but to give way; sure, never a man did the same with a worse grace since the beginning of thwarting.

Truly, it seemed as circumstance were bent on justifying every word Mr. Browning had said, that morning; for in the first place, our men being marched under arms to the barn-door, the Irishmen made no more resistance than dust to the broom; nay, they showed even some alacrity to be gone. Further, being arrived at the outermost gate, and our men being halted, the leader (for it goes against the grain with me to call so scurvy a creature captain) turned back and craved a word apart with Mr. Browning. One may doubt if there be honour, but of a surety there is gratitude even in the breast of a thief.

'Sir,' said he, 'I'd fain make some return for your entertainment; and so I warn ye that as soon as the Earl comes to the front, information will be laid of you being in your own house. There was a talk last night of laying hold of you ourselves, but some of us were against it, and the rest judged themselves not strong enough to face your servants. But take my advice now, and get you gone to some hiding-place before your retreat be cut off; if ye can, even now, for the country's full of bands of Antrim's.'

Mr. Browning stared at him blankly; presently he burst out laughing.

'If I don't believe he takes me for Captain

Hamilton,' said he, 'may I be whipt! Why, my good man, I am none of him, but one that is his friend, sure enough—ask this man my name.'

'Captain Browning,' said Cargill, at once, 'of the ship *Mountjoy.*'

''Ods nails!' said the other; 'and so you may be, an it like you; and so I have my pains for my thanks!'

And at that he turned his back on them, and left them, looking pernicious sour.

Mr. Browning lost no time in conveying this caution to the ears it was meant for, as soon as he was returned to the house; it gave some colour of likelihood—even over-much—to his fear that we might be beset, later in the day, by a larger force. But as to flying, while yet there was time, Captain Hamilton scouted the thought.

'Here I am,' said he, 'and here I bide; let him that can lay his hand on me possess his fortune!'

Nor could we move him from this resolve.

'No,' said he. 'Had it not been for the trusty friendship of yourself and your wife, Browning, mine had been left alone to face as ugly an adventure as could happen to any lady. I conceive it more my duty, now that dirty times are threatening, to look to the welfare of my household than to take care of mine own worthless skin.'

Mr. Canning added his persuasion to ours, without effect. Captain Hamilton had in this matter a ready answer to everything that could be brought up to turn him to our way of thinking.

'And you shall understand,' said he at last, 'that I count it far less dangerous to stay here than to fly across the country, so infested as they say it is—and I believe it—with marauding bands of Ultoghs. I shall be well disguised, never fear; and do you think there's one among the men that would betray me? Ask Cargill.'

'Well, and that's true enough,' said I; 'but there's that groom of Mr. Phillips', can anyone answer for him, do ye think? or for any other dastard?'

'Very likely not,' said Captain Hamilton coolly. 'But we can take a hint from what you did last night, and try what the fear of a pistol will be like for a gag to him. Oh! never you fear, my friends. I know too well the value of my life to *risk it*, riding abroad in so unsettled a time. But truly,' said he mighty seriously, a minute after, 'I much fear that it will be needful that you ladies should face that same danger. 'Twere more to my mind than a present of a thousand pound, if one would set you both down in the Diamond of Derry this minute.'

'What!' said I, with indignation, 'and leave

you here at Cloncally? Sure, if 'tis a thing
disgraceful and cowardly for you, 'tis nothing
better for me, and you shall not ask it of me if
you love me.'

Dear! but there was a fine storm of talk
round mine ears the next minute, nor could I
so much as pretend to shut them to what was
said. They fell to describing how Cloncally
might straightway be surrounded by hordes of
wild Ultoghs from the hills, bent on slaughter;
how Derry at least was safe, being forewarned;
and how, the women and children being out of
danger, the hands of the men were set free
from much hindrance, both in defence and in
sally. They were all in one story, and Mrs.
Browning joined them.

'What would you have given,' said she, 'to
know that your son Roland was in perfect
safety last night? The thought of my grand-
child Mary was a very tower of strength to me,
I can tell you.'

'And yet,' said I, 'you so ill endured the
thought of your husband in peril that you came
forth out of the same safety to be by his side.'

The tears that come to me so seldom stood
in mine eyes from pure vexation; 'twas my
turn now to chafe at the friendship that urged
me—for mine own good—to do a thing so distasteful to me. But of what use was chafing

when Captain Hamilton had made up his mind?
As well may the taken fish chafe against the
net. He went to and fro, hastening the preparations for our departure.

'Nay, nay,' said he, when I desired time to
make some necessary arrangements, as I
thought them; 'you are even too long here
already. Hasten—hasten, if you have any
care for my peace of mind.'

And so had us all presently on horseback,
and on the road to Derry, each behind an
armed man (himself was my groom, dressed
in a suit of his own livery), and with two others
in front of the party, and two behind, as our
escort.

We had ridden but a little way—not a mile,
nor anything like it — when we overtook a
party of loiterers, no doubt belonging to the
party that had lain over-night in our own barn;
they eyed us in a mighty unfriendly manner.
To be sure, they were scarce likely to know
the party for some of their entertainers, never
having seen any of the women, nor any of the
gentlemen save Mr. Browning. Moreover, we
rode fast, and passed them at a trot.

Ever the further we went, the more of the
Rapparees we fell in with. As we drew near
to the Waterside, the road was alive with them.
'Twas a plain impossibility to get at the ferry,

which we judged must be in their own hands. Whether it was so or no, it was clear that both ferry and ferrymen must be altogether in their power, and in such a case to attempt the crossing would have been but to offer them a prey.

There was no need for a council among our defenders, as, indeed, there was no time.

'Back again!' said Captain Hamilton, Mr. Browning, and Mr. Canning with one accord.

They turned their horses as smartly as if they had been drilled to it, and we took the homeward road at the same pace we kept in going—to wit, a trot that was smart enough for business, but had no appearance of flight.

Yet the mere fact of retreat doth bring the mind into a state of apprehension, and it seemed to me that these very men who had permitted us to pass unmolested on our way towards the city seemed now as they had fain stopped us had they had but the time to make up their minds. Whether the others observed the same or no, I cannot say; they kept on at the same even trot, passing the bands of the Red-shank soldiers without so much as a glance at them over the shoulder.

They might be minded to stop us, but to attempt it was beyond their courage (we riding so compact), till we came to the stretch of level road that lies about half a mile from Cloncally gate. Here were a goodly number of the Ultoghs, scattered in parties of threes and fours; they saw our band while it was yet at some distance, and ran together with one consent. This was a motion that, in such circumstances, carried a threat. Captain Hamilton held up his hand for a halt; he had assumed the command of the party, little as command accorded with his disguise.

'Will they attempt to stop us, think you?' said he.

'Devil a doubt of it,' said Mr. Canning, dropping into his fighting manners. 'It's yourself they're after, too; they're aware of the reward that's set upon you.'

'But they're not acquaint with your person,' said Mr. Browning, 'and in that dress they need never suspect you.'

'Very good,' said Captain Hamilton; 'then the less is the risk of the plan I offer.' And so explained it to them in a very few words, there being not a moment to lose. As it always is with him, it was the post of danger he claimed, nor would he be said 'Nay' to. Neither was there time for discussion, for who knew but more of the Ultoghs might draw together to strengthen those that stood already in two close ranks across the road? I was very speedily helped from my pillion, and

remounted behind Timothy the groom ; Roland
in my lap, for I feared lest the gallop might
shake the child from his seat in front of the
saddle. Captain Hamilton and Mr. Canning
then rid forward with one of the armed
servants ; we followed as close as we could in
two rows of three, the outermost men of the
hinder rank being the armed servants that at
first had been our rear-guard.

'Ready ?' said my husband, turning in his
stirrups. 'Then follow me, and do as I do;
remember that 'twill be well if we can avoid
harming these scullogues that have the King's
commission among them.'

At that he set forward at a gentle trot, the
rest keeping pace and place. Being come to
within an hundred yards of the Irishmen, he
stands up in his stirrups once more.

'Now,' says he. And we all dashed forward
at a charging pace. But being come to within
twenty paces of the foe, for so undoubtedly
they were, suddenly he swerved to the left,
where the ground was sound and the galloping
safe. The Irish, who are as quick as the light
in their wits, were after us in an instant to
head us off; but they stood at a disadvantage,
being across the road, and there were no more
than a dozen that had the least chance of
throwing themselves in our way. Of these,

not one man dared to stand his ground when they came nigh to the naked swords, but quailed and stood aside ; so raw and undisciplined were the men that were thought fit to take the place of Mountjoy's veterans. Sure, had there been but one man among them with the soldier's gift, he had shown them how to choose ground for their stand against us where it was less easy to evade them.

By the time we were nearing the broken ground that lies just around Cloncally, those that pursued us (for there were some that had the wit to try to head us off by the road, seeing that we must make a circuit to regain it) were left far behind. But there was little time to lose, for all that. We rid into the courtyard nigh as far spent as Mr. Phillips' groom the morning before ; 'twas a fortunate thing for us that every man of our little force was made of other stuff than he. They needed scarce a word of command, but had the gate of the courtyard shut before a man of our pursuers was in sight round the corner ; the front of the house was done ere we came within doors, Cargill having taken fright at the sound of our over-speedy approach.

Mrs. Browning and I stood with the child and the maids, just within the house. Mine ears were on the stretch for the clamour of our pursuers at the gate. The men were busying themselves with the horses, gentle as well as simple lending a hand to put them into the stable out of the way. Suddenly there was a kind of cry from Captain Hamilton:

'Dear God!' said he, 'there's one of us missing. Who is it?'

''Tis Captain Browning, sir, an it like you,' said Timothy the groom, raising himself from beside a horse he was ungirthing. 'He turned about and rid back through the gate as soon as ever he had dismounted his lady.'

'And you said nothing to me, sirrah!' said my husband, his eyes flashing.

'Nay, sir, how was it my duty?' said Timothy. 'Sure, I knew not but you marked him.'

Captain Hamilton turned from him to Mrs. Browning for an explanation, his face as pale as the dead. She was nigh as white as he, but perfectly collected.

'I would beg you to take it with composure, sir,' said she. ''Tis a plan my husband hath thought of. I hope it may turn to good.'

Briefly, the plan was this: Mr. Browning knew that it was he that was thought to be Captain Hamilton. He knew also that 'twas for the sake of the reward set upon his apprehension that the soldiers sought to take that gentleman; needs must he, therefore, be brought

before the Earl of Antrim, their Colonel. Now,
Mr. Browning was known by sight to my lord,
as; indeed, was Captain Hamilton also. His
plan was to avert from us the danger of an
attack by suffering the soldiers to take him
without more ado. Captain Hamilton was for
riding forth at once, and giving himself up.

'Open the gates, there!' shouted he to the
men; and was a-buckling of his girths again,
when Mr. Canning caught him by the arm. I
also laid hold of him. Mrs. Browning stood by
him.

'Hear reason, Hamilton,' said Mr. Canning.
'Of what use were it that you should throw
away your liberty—perhaps your life?'

'Sir!' exclaimed my husband, in a flame, 'do
you think I'd allow another man to stand in my
danger? Never, sir! You should answer me
for the base, unworthy thought, had I the time
to demand satisfaction.'

'Nay, do but listen to me, sir,' besought Mrs.
Browning, at his elbow. ''Tis a small danger
Mr. Browning runs—scarce to be reckoned;
my lord the Earl knows him; he will be set at
liberty as soon as he is seen. For you it were
nothing short of death. Nay, sir; if you think,
as you said this morning, that we have shown
you any friendship in this matter, do not refuse
us this favour. Be ruled, and stay in your own

house until you shall know that your surrendering yourself shall serve some good purpose.'

'Mary,' said my husband, 'speak you for me : you would not have me disgraced.'

But Mrs. Browning took him by the hand.

'I ask it as an especial favour,' said she. ''Tis my husband's scheme ; do not balk it, I pray you.'

'Twas a bitter pill to Captain Hamilton.

'Madam,' said he, 'I dare not refuse you. Sure, you know not what you have asked of me.' And so fell mighty sadly to grooming of his horse.

CHAPTER XV.

HOW LORD ANTRIM HIMSELF AND HIS STAFF CAME TO CLONCALLY.

To myself, though I was sorry for my husband's grief, and anxious to boot on behalf of his friend, 'twas like coming within a very haven of refuge to return within the walls of mine own house. It had been so sorely against my will that I had left it, two hours ago. My household of two, Annot Wilson and Margery, were entirely of the same mind, and fell to their work with a far better will than they had left it, beginning at once to prepare fresh victual, whereof there was · a notable lack in the larder.

So passed the day, and after it the night, without the least molestation or any circumstance to revive our fear. Captain Hamilton chafed mightily; but, Lord! what use was in chafing? For my own part, peace seemed to settle down on my heart, so that I found myself going about the house with a snatch of song upon my lips.

Alas! the time for peace and for singing was
yet far off in the future; and so, before the
sun was high next morning, I was harshly
reminded.

For going with my son into his nursery (I
being now, by force of circumstances, become
his nurse), I stepped to the window to look out.
Sure, I know not what I thought to see; but
that window looks upon the courtyard, and
gives likewise, in the distance, the prospect of
a part of the road to Derry. The courtyard
below me was silent and empty; but when
I looked towards the city, the road was thronged
with a crowd of men that were making towards
Cloncally.

Here was a portent that I knew not how to
interpret. I ran to tell, first Mrs. Browning
(for it did pass through my mind that perhaps,
discovering who her husband really was, this
mob was escorting him back to Cloncally), and
then Mr. Canning and Captain Hamilton. But
by the time they were come to the window, the
press was gone out of sight in the hollows;
only a few stragglers were scattered here and
there upon the road. James and Mr. Canning
scanned them curiously.

'They be fugitives, I fear,' said Captain
Hamilton.

'Manifest fugitives,' said Mr. Canning. 'You

can plainly see it in their gait, even at this distance.'

'Then God have mercy upon Derry,' said Captain Hamilton, 'for I fear 'tis in an evil case!'

Whereat Mrs. Browning, at his elbow, groaned aloud in the bitterness of her heart.

'But there are some that have escaped, as we see,' said he, trying to offer her some small crumb of comfort. 'We can shelter the poor souls here, God be praised! though it be,' he added in a lower voice, 'but till our own turn come.'

And so was turning from the window to bid throw open the courtyard gates to the flying crowd, whom we nothing doubted to be the poor people that had fled from the massacre. But Mr. Canning counselled caution.

'Sure,' said he, 'where's the hurry? Wait until you see them closer. There's not a man of the pursuers in sight yet. Besides——'

And there he stopped, not saying what was 'besides'; only he peered over the hollows as though he would fain draw up a sight of the fugitives to the tops of the trees.

His eyesight, methinks, must have been marvellous clear, and that same clear eyesight was our salvation, no less. For presently, when some of the foremost came stumbling into view,

here were no sober citizens, terrified out of their
grave wits, but Antrim's Red-shanks, back again
upon our hands, coming the same way they had
gone, but at a mighty different rate. Spite
of their flagging gait, they carried all the marks
of desperate men in their savage, terror-stricken
visages, and hustling, stumbling flight. 'Twas
as if they ran in fetters, and heard the lash of
their pursuers whistling over their heads ; and
though the fetters were nought but weariness
and fear, yet they seemed to lie as heavy on
their limbs as any chain.

The foremost passed the turning of the road
in their blind terror, but some that followed
took it ; then both those that had been before
them, and those that came after, crowded
behind them into the narrower road, like the
meeting waters of two rivers in flood. 'Twas a
fearsome sight, and worse instead of better the
closer they came.

Those that were close in front of the house
were out of sight from the window where
we stood ; but it needed not the view of them
to cramp my heart with fear. Their clamour
was so savage that 'twas shocking. 'Twas
not their shouts, which were scarce more than
a hoarse murmur, their breath was so spent ;
but though they scarce could stand, they
beat upon the great gate of the court with a

most terrible passion, as men that would tear
it from its posts before it should shut them from
the safety they thought to lie behind it. My
knees were weak beneath me to hear them.
For desperate men are no better than wild
beasts ; you may restrain Leviathan as soon as
them.

Up above them, at the window, we held a
hasty council of war, the question being, who
should conduct the parley that was not to
be avoided. 'Twas still being debated, when
Mrs. Browning, with a little cry, drew our
attention to the distant road, where was come
in view a travelling coach, escorted by a
company of horsemen, whose accoutrements
flashed and sparkled as they rode. Such a
sight were rare enough at Cloncally on any
day and at any season to engross our wonder
and attention ; but on a day in the dark month
of December, and at a time when so disquiet-
ing rumours were everywhere abroad, 'twas
veritably a sight to set one staring and mar-
velling like any rustic.

The question, ' Who can it be ?' that sprang
to the lips of all of us, could have but one
answer. There was but one person that was
likely to be abroad in his coach at such a
time—but one person that was like to be so
attended on his travels ; and that person was

my lord the Earl of Antrim, who might well
be on his way by this time to take up his
command in Derry; and something of the
tardiest, too, when one came to consider it.

So we said to each other, clean forgetting the
clamorous mob below in this new interest. It
could be no one else than my lord the Earl, we
were agreed.

'But—grant me patience!' said my husband,
as the coach went out of view in the hollows,
'how comes the man so far out of his way if his
way be to his command in Derry? There's
something here that is beyond my skill to
fathom.'

'He's after his runaways, no doubt,' said
Mr. Canning.

'And a mercy for us if he be,' I rejoined,
taking note again how the noise from the
courtyard below was grown since the rabble
were rested.

I can scarce credit mine own memory, and so
can scarce hope to be believed when I record
what is nevertheless the plain truth—to wit,
that these varlets, beginning to find strength
and breath after their flight, made so great a
riot in front of the house as to drown the noise
of the approaching coach with its escort. My
Lord of Antrim dropped upon them utterly at
unawares, *like a bolt out of a clear sky*, as the

saying is, and they being taken by surprise, and
my lord's person unknown to them, he stood in
some danger of being mishandled among them.
But the gentlemen that were his escort—a company of as gallant persons as ever I set eyes on
—fell to laying about them with a very good
will, so that the rabble gave back from the door
and let the coach come up.

By the time the pages had let the steps
down, Cargill had opened the door to the
newcomers, all the while beseeching his master,
who for once, was ready to take his counsel, to
bethink him of his disguise and of the jeopardy
he stood in, and to permit me to do the honours
of the house as though he were not present. I
even put myself forward without his leave, and
stood just within the porch, supported by Mrs.
Browning and Mr. Canning upon my right and
left, to receive these new guests that fortune,
bad or good, had sent me.

Sure, it seemed as the great coach were never
to be unladed of them that were in it. A gentleman had descended or ever the house-door was
opened ; him I knew not. Then came another
that I knew and was glad in my heart to see—
namely, Colonel Phillips, of Newtown-Lima-
vady. After him came a gentlewoman I had
never seen before ; and after her my Lord of
Antrim, something high in his colour and

black in his looks, which was little marvel, considering the behaviour of his men. After him came another gentlewoman, with a pair of merry dark eyes of her own that seemed to take in everything at a single sweeping glance—us who waited in the doorway, the gentlemen that by this time were dismounted, and the mob that peeped and scowled behind. Methought that there was little mirth in these same black bright eyes as she turned them on the last; but then she faced towards the coach again, as the rest had done (all but my lord), and waited.

Then one of the pages fetched out a little jackanapes that mopped and mowed in a velvet coat and cap, like a child's. The other brought out a little lapdog wrapped in a costly shawl. These curious passengers were handed to the two waiting-gentlewomen to hold, who took them with the same care and reverence as if they had been human beings and my lord's children.

Next after these came my lord's confessor, a veritable Jack Priest, in cassock and tonsure, that held up his two fingers and blessed the company in the Latin tongue as they bowed to him in the deepest reverence. For mine own part, having no mind to disguise my faith, I gave him no more than the merest ordinary curtsey—scarce that—when his turn came to be presented to me.

But that was not until the last and greatest of this aristocratical company was descended from her coach—to wit, my lady Countess of Antrim, with a face of vinegar, and a voice that matched it for sourness, as she inquired of her jackanapes and her lapdog, before ever she condescended to receive the greetings of her hostess, 'How they did, the little sweethearts, and whether they were wearied to death by the jolting of the nasty coach.' Never in my life did I hear trifling that matched so ill with the voice and aspect of her that uttered it. Sure, it threw a new light upon the reason why his regiment went so ill-clad and so undisciplined, to see their Colonel and commander so wrapped up in his priest, and his wife, and his wife's antics; for there he stood in the doorway, waiting with the submission of a lackey till her ladyship should have ended her tendernesses with her pets, before he should take leave to offer her his hand and lead her into the house.

My lady lifted a pair of scrutinizing eyes upon me (who had often been in company with her before), and feigned to have a difficulty in calling my name to mind, wherein my lord was her prompter. And I, on my part, was a little

put to it, between irritation and amusement, to
find words to inquire for her ladyship's health
that should not seem a mere paraphrase of hers
to her animals—nay, the impulse took me to
repeat them word for word. It had been so
comical a jest, save for its insolence, to have
inquired of this acid and disdainful lady, ' How
she did, the pretty sweetheart, and whether she
were tired to death by the jolting of the nasty
coach.'

Mastering this temptation, I made a shift to
receive the Countess in a manner befitting
alike her rank and my breeding, presenting
Mrs. Browning both to her and to her gentlewomen, so soon as these latter had been made
known to myself.

Yet it cost me no small effort to force
my mind to these small courtesies. Can the
compass-needle point to the written north upon
the chart, when the true north lies another
way? My true north was without among
the grooms and lackeys, where stood my husband close to a dozen men that knew his
person perfectly well. I looked, every moment,
to hear some gentleman speak to him by his
name, and ask him what he did in the clothes
he wore. And yet the best thing I could do
for him was to show no sign of misgiving, or of
any interest in him. Being caught where he

was, sure, unconcern was his best policy, and
boldness his only safety ; and to discharge the
service of a groom as though 'twere the merest
matter of course.

It seemed as if we were never to come within
doors, there was so much questioning and
answering, and talk of the great portent, that so
many men of my lord Earl's were here upon
the road when they should have been there in
the city. But presently, as some of the fugitives
were brought forward to be questioned by their
Colonel, my lady Countess signified her pleasure
to leave them and go into the house, and so
we did.

My eyes, taking the line of Mrs. Browning's, caught sight of her husband among the
gentlemen of my Lord of Antrim's following—
a welcome sight. It was hard to go out of
view of mine, and to know nothing of what
befell him; for if once he were noticed, I thought
to myself, he were as good as arrested ; and if
once arrested, as good as imprisoned and
executed.

I was busy endeavouring to satisfy my Lady
Antrim's questions (sure, to hear the turn she
gave them, anyone had thought I was responsible
for the safe entry of the troops into the city),
when my lord enters to us, with a few of his
gentlemen.

' Here's a pretty kettle of fish, indeed, in the city !' says he, very much ruffled.

·'And what is the new trouble ?' asks my lady, drawing her brows together. I promise you that she but put the question that was trembling on every lip.

''Tis neither more nor less than flat rebellion,' says my lord ; ' an overt resistance—ay, and an armed resistance—of the King's troops ! 'Twill be a hanging business for the ringleaders, I nothing doubt, unless the King's temper be changed to that of a dove by all his troubles. Figure it, ladies ! My foremost company present themselves duly at the city gates yester-day, showing the King's potent, as, of course, it was right they should. Before the Mayor can have taken time so much as to read it, my men find the gate shut in their faces, and them-selves menaced with violence, if they make not the speedier retreat.'

' That's old news !' said my Lady Antrim fretfully. ' It happened o' Friday. What else turned us from the road to the town, I'd like to ask ? It's something newer, I'll warrant, that hath set them scampering for their lives to-day —ay, and something fiercer ! What's the new treason ?' Then she turned her eyes on me, for all the world as though she blamed me for the whole coil and confusion. ' Upon my word,' says she, 'it passes the limits of belief that sober citizens should comport themselves so unruly.'

The blood rushed to my cheeks at her folly, as of a child, that must ever have someone to blame for any mischance.

'Credible or no,' says my lord, 'Mrs. Hamilton is but too competent a witness of its truth.' Here he makes me a pretty bow, adding a word or two of thanks for the timely succour I had afforded to his men. 'Why should they be here craving a bite to eat and leave to creep under a roof for the night,' he continued, 'if they were free to go into Derry, where they had a right to both quarters and rations? The thing speaks for itself.'

'Ah, my Lord Antrim!' said I to him, 'sure I am as anxious as your lady to know what the new fright is to-day. Did they ask admittance again this morning? If they did, we were mighty near being of their company. And were they repulsed a second time, and if so, in what manner? What thing in the world could be done to them to put them in such a frenzy as we saw?'

My Lord Antrim broke out a-laughing, though in no very mirthful key.

'Of a truth, Mrs. Hamilton,' said he, 'your questions crowd so fast upon each other that

I'm at a loss to answer them all. Ask admittance? I dare say they did, though these fellows below said nothing of it, that I can call to mind. Their story was as confused and as halting as mine is like to be—ill hearing makes ill rehearsing. But as far as I can make out, they were loitering around the town and the Waterside this morning, awaiting my coming, when all on a sudden comes a train-band out of the city, and begins to draw up in the order of attack; and at the same time, to catch them between two foes, comes a troop of horse over the hills from Glendermot. The men they might have faced, perhaps, though attacked upon two sides at once; but the city guards began to turn their ordnance upon them, and that undid them quite. Poor fellows! 'twas little marvel if they fled; they have had small chance yet of learning the sound of sakers and demi-culverins. Whether they were pursued or no, I can't make out by their own telling; and that is strange, for, sure, anyone would say that they must have been, and that most furiously, to fall into such a panic.'

'Are any of them hurt, do you know?' I inquired.

'Why, none of those down in the courtyard,' said he. 'But that's the strange thing; they can't tell me of any wounds. To be sure, wounded men cannot run very far ; they will be found nearer Derry, no doubt.' Then he falls a-smiling in a sort of embarrassed fashion. ' I can't conceal from myself,' says he, ' that I am like to have but little credit of my regiment— at least, until they've seen some service, and are hardened. And now,' says he, look- ing round upon us, ' what think you of such behaviour from a town reputed loyal and peace- able ?'

Again my Lady Antrim made herself the spokeswoman for the rest of us.

'If I tell you what I think, my lord,' said she, ' I fear 'twill be but little to your liking.'

' Never spare for that, my love,' said he, with an odd little grimace and a bow. Plainly, it was no uncommon thing for this lady to make speeches that were not to the liking of her lord.

' I am wondering, then,' said she, very cold and precise, ' whether your lordship can conceal from yourself that the blame lies as much with you as with them ? Had you in person pre- sented the potent, the town had never dreamed of disputing it ; you can't deny that. Let us hope,' continued she, still more lofty and exact, ' that this blunder will be a lesson to you. Let us hope that another time you will give ear to those friends who tell you that the commander of a regiment ought to march along with it.'

I pitied my Lord Antrim, who looked mighty uneasy.

'Surely,' I exclaimed, 'there's little wisdom in portioning out the blame at this hour of the day. What's done, is done, and can't be mended ; but no doubt some arrangement can be made, if 'twere set about in a proper way.'

My lady Countess gave me a look that was designed to bring me to a sense of my temerity; but, faith, I never dropped mine eyes. She was no wife of mine, that I should quail before her disapproval, like my poor Lord Antrim, who had never a word to say to my suggestion. But one of the gentlemen that rode with him, my Lord McGuire of Enniskillen, took it up very heartily.

'That's extremely well said of you, Mrs. Hamilton,' said he. 'There's not a bit of wisdom in crying over spilt milk. There must be something fit to be done to set matters to rights. The thing is, to make up our minds what it is, and then to do it.'

'And if I may take leave to express my opinion,' said another gentleman, whom they called Colkitto (I think he was one of the Mac-Donnels of that place, and, indeed, there were

some of the gallantest men in the North of
Ireland that rode by my Lord Antrim's side in
this ill-managed affair)—'if I may take leave to
express my opinion,' says he, 'it would be that
the first thing is to get trustworthy news from
Derry. Does not your lordship think so?'

'In faith, I do!' said Lord Antrim ruefully.
'But who's to get it for us? For I shrewdly
fear that any man that's known to be my
envoy may whistle for entrance into Derry.
Do but think of it!'

At this there arose a perfect competition
among the gentlemen that were in the room
for the errand, each one pressing his services
upon my lord; the touch of danger that was
thought to lie in it added fuel, as it were, to
their eagerness. 'Twas impossible not to admire
such a spirit; and it did flash through one's
mind at the same time, that if all this gallantry
had been at the head of the regiment instead of
at the tail, the men had been like to show a
better spirit and to behave with greater firmness.

Mr. Phillips, our neighbour, had said mighty
little all this time, though listening to every
word. Presently he stepped forward to my
lord, and began to speak; and as he spoke, the
others fell to listening.

'My lord,' said he, 'it is perfectly true that
any man that is known to come from you will

have some difficulty to get into Derry at present. Would your lordship accept of my services as an envoy, for the townsmen have long known me for a friend of theirs, as you are no doubt aware? As one that knows their grievances and the reason for their conduct to your troops, I think they would have confidence in me.'

My Lord Antrim all but gasped in his surprise.

'What, sir!' said he. 'You know their reasons for it, and their grievances, and you have forborne to tell us of them! How is this? Sure, if we know what they'd be at, we are half-way through our difficulties!'

Mr. Phillips in his turn looked astonished.

'But surely, my lord,' said he, 'you can't be ignorant of the trouble yourself. You know the state of distraction the whole country's gone into since the news of the massacre went abroad.'

'Massacre! What massacre?' asked Lord Antrim quickly. 'You surely don't mean this ridiculous story that's got abroad in the last two days of a rising among the Catholics to attack the Protestants? You don't mean to tell me that there's any man of station or of judgment that believes it?'

Now again it was the turn of Mr. Phillips to be surprised. He and my Lord Antrim, in this

colloquy, they bandied astonishment between
them as if 'twere a game of ball they were
engaged in.

'Why, my lord,' said he, ''tis a cordial to
hear you mention it in that tone of contempt.
But as to believing it, you may take my word
there's not a man, woman, or child in Derry but
is at least as sure of it as he is of his creed.'

'There's a gentleman below,' said Lord
McGuire—'he that met us upon the road.
He, I mean, that was brought to your lordship
by the name of Captain Hamilton, of Cloncally,
and was known to be none of him as soon as
you clapped eyes on him. He is of the city,
isn't he?'

'To be sure!' said my lord. 'Desire him to
have the kindness to step this way, will you?
I'd like to hear more of this madness from one
that hath been in the thick of it.'

Mr. Browning gave him no long time to
wait, but was with him upon the moment with
my Lord McGuire, two or three more coming
with them, so that my room began to show like
a guard-room. Being questioned by my Lord o
Antrim, Mr. Browning gave a very circumstantial account of the terror and indignation
that were felt in the city; at which hearing my
lord professed himself more astonished than
ever, and deeply shocked and grieved at the

mischief wrought by a foolish and heartless joke ; for it was thus he spoke of the famous letter to my Lord Mount-Alexander, that had been the beginning of all the alarm.

Mr. Browning stood and listened very gravely to all this tirade. Then he lifted his eyes very considerately upon my lord, who had wrought himself up into something of a rapture.

'I understand your lordship to speak of this rumour as perfectly false ?' said he.

'The most bottomless rubbish, sir !' said my lord. 'False and foolish as if the father of lies was the author of it !'

'And how,' said Mr. Browning, 'can you bring your mind to think so ?'

Here was a sudden turning of the tables. My lord, I thought, would fain have blustered ; but there was that in Mr. Browning's manner that compelled a courteous answer. He paused for some moments, however, looking from one to another of his company, as though he pondered their tempers and how far it were prudent to speak his mind in their hearing.

'Sir,' said he at last, 'I'll be better able to answer your doubts if you'll tell me how they've been bred and nourished. What could suggest the thought of such treachery—what could make it seem even possible—I own I'm at a loss to conceive.'

If that were so (and, sure, one has no right to doubt it, though it presents my lord as a mere blind bat in his politics, and a man of a singular forgetfulness in his history), he was presently very thoroughly enlightened. Mr. Browning made him no long speech, but in a very few words he laid before him the main grounds of the apprehension and mistrust that were so rife among the Protestants of the province. The disarming of the Englishry ; the arming of the Irishry, even to the lower orders ; the discharge of the Protestants from the King's troops, and the filling up of their places with undisciplined Irish ; the arrogance of the Irish throughout the province for months past ; the exhortations of their priests, and the prospects of power and of vengeance that they did not stick to hold out to their people—it passes my wit to recall how, in so few words, he made the whole black catalogue stand out so living and so clear. And not a word that was overstrong for courtesy to my lord's Catholic prejudices, only the simple and exact statement of facts that were within the knowledge of every man in the room. My Lord Antrim's countenance and demeanour altered mightily as he listened.

'Sir,' said he, when Mr. Browning had finished, 'I own that what you say throws a complete new light on circumstances that, taken one by one, are innocent enough. Will you accept my assurance that the appearance they have of being parts of a design or plot against you is purely accidental? There was no harm whatever intended to the Protestants of Ulster. I speak from knowledge, sir,' he ended very seriously.

Mr. Browning looked straight and earnestly at my lord as he spoke, as one that hath a mind to fathom him that would persuade him, even to the bottom of his soul—ay, and that is able to do it; discerning not merely whether the man be speaking as he thinks, but whether he be of the quality which sees the thing that is. My lord could not be unconscious that he was being weighed and valued.

'Why, sir,' said he, 'don't you take me? There may be reasons in plenty why his Majesty may desire to have as many of his loyal subjects under arms—men he can depend on—you follow me?—as ever he may. I regret I can't be plainer, for you seem a civil gentleman enough, and a man of singular discretion; but I hope you'll take my word for it.'

Mr. Browning bowed.

'Certainly, my Lord Antrim,' said he. 'I have not the smallest doubt but you speak as you believe, and out of what you are entitled to consider certain knowledge.'

'Why, sir,' exclaimed my lord, 'don't you know that I'm of the Council of State? What more would you have?'

This time Mr. Browning paused before he answered. For certainly 'tis a serious matter for one gentleman to appear to doubt a thing that another hath affirmed of his knowledge.

'Perhaps,' said he, 'I have already presumed too far upon your lordship's patience.'

'Not a bit, indeed!' said Lord Antrim. 'On the contrary, you do me a favour when you instruct me where the shoe pinches here in the North.'

But though his words were so courteous, there was a certain expectancy in his manner, as of one that thought his honour impugned, and would not suffer the subject to pass till it were righted. And long ere this, the attention of every man in the room was fixed upon the conversation between him and Mr. Browning, who, on his part, replied at once, and frankly, though with a very evident sense of the difficulty he was in.

'My lord Earl,' said he, 'for your own goodwill towards us—for your own personal intentions—for your interpretation of the intentions of those at the head of affairs—you have said enough, and more than enough. If I can't profess myself entirely reassured on every

point, I hope your lordship will take into consideration that all circumstances, for months,
have conspired together to raise our suspicions
in certain high quarters ; to that degree that it
is not easy to suppose them candid, even with
their own colleagues, if these should have any
friendship towards us.'

'If the gentleman glances at the Lord
Deputy, there,' broke in a certain Colonel
Talbot that was in the room, and that is said to
be nearer akin to the said Lord Deputy than he
can very well own to, ' I'll be happy to give
him a lesson in faith and in manners at the
same time !' And with that, he clapt his hand
upon his sword-hilt in a very meaning way.

My Lord Antrim raised his hand.

'Sir,' said he, ' I'd have you to remember
where you are, and in what presence ; such
offers are not fit for ladies' ears, sir. And I'd
have you to remember, besides, that no names
were named, sir—better follow a good example,
and let them remain unspoken. As to your
doubt, sir,' and here he turned to Mr. Browning
with a deal of dignity—it sat well on him too,
and showed him to far greater advantage than
his former manner—'as I all but forced you to
speak it, I must even pocket the affront. But
give me leave to assure you, on the word of a
gentleman, that I speak not as I *think*, but as I

know. Your massacre is a *hoax*, sir, an ill-contrived and spiteful jest—nothing more. And that you will presently see for yourself.' And so bowed to Mr. Browning to terminate the conversation.

'I thank your lordship for that assurance, which I am happy to be able to accept,' said he, bowing very low; 'and I beg you will pardon any discourtesy I may have been led into, which I should deeply regret, indeed.'

'Say no more, sir; you said nothing blame-worthy,' he replied; and so turned towards Mr. Phillips. 'Sir,' he said to him, 'may I beg you will convey the same assurance to your fellow-townsmen? for I do think you are the fittest man to go between me and the town; and it is no disparagement to any of you, gentlemen,' said he, addressing those that had been so eager for the office, 'neither to your courage nor your discretion, you being under a disadvantage that he is free from.'

No sooner was this decided, than I saw Mr. Browning slip quietly from the room. 'Ah, good friend and true,' thought I with a gush of gratitude at the heart, 'you go to send my husband out of danger.'

And so it was. For when Mr. Phillips was departing, I could not forbear to excuse myself to my lady Countess, and go to the window to see him start, as, indeed, did many of the rest, for the windows were full of spectators. And sure enough, Captain Hamilton rid among his servants. He lifted his eyes to the windows, and scanned them for a sight of me; I knew it, and drew back, lest any inadvertence should betray him. And as I did so, sure, my very soul fell a-trembling, to see upon a sudden the narrowness of his escape. For what think you? At the very next window were two with their heads together, and another leaning upon their shoulders. They were talking in a low tone; but I promise you I caught every word, for my ears were sharpened by my painful fear.

''Tis he, I tell you,' said one; 'I thought so when he stood by my horse's head, below there, and now I'm sure of it.'

'What fools we were to let such a chance slip through our fingers!' said another. 'It's not too late now, if we were to ride after them.'

'And share the credit—and the reward to boot—with a dozen others that would stick their fingers into our pie!' said the first. 'No, no, my friend; have patience but for a short hour or two, and we shall have him safe enough when he returns from Derry.'

'What ails you against the poor fellow?' asked the man who leant over their shoulders. 'He never did you any ill. And, after all, what's a likeness? A groom resembles his master—well, what's more likely? He may have been *born in the family*, like one, that is in company, in my Lord Deputy's.'

And so, with a laugh and a wicked sneer, turned on his heel, and left them.

But judge if I prayed in my heart that my husband might have the prudence to remain in Derry, as I sat and talked trifles with my lady Countess and her suite.

CHAPTER XVI.

HOW IT WAS RESOLVED TO QUIT CLONCALLY FOR DERRY.

SURE, there were little interest in a circumstantial relation of what we did to pass away the hours until Mr. Phillips should be returned from Derry. The said hours were none so many, after all, and that was a very great and signal mercy; for they were some of the most tedious that ever I passed in my life. Lord! what a burden is the company of a great lady that hath no manners.

And yet, perhaps it is scarce justice to charge upon my Lady Antrim's haughtiness the whole weariness of the waiting, for, certes, there was none of us but had a heart full of trouble or of fear to turn every minute into sixty. 'Tis a true saying, that everything comes to an end at last, if one will but have patience; and would be most encouraging, if one could but realize it at the moment of need. But truly, that after-

noon, it might well have seemed as though our
lives should come to their end in the meantime,
and there had been little enough satisfaction in
that.

When at last it was known that Mr. Phillips
was kept by force in Derry, with his servants, I
clean forgot my weariness in my joy, for now
was my husband safe. I could have shouted
aloud for very gladness, and so have smothered
other noises which were less profitable and less
pleasant—I mean my Lord Antrim's railing,
and my lady's drops of vinegar venom upon his
wounded dignity. For when the messenger
delivered the errand he was charged with—to
wit, a flat refusal on the part of the city to
admit either my lord himself or any of his
company within the gates—he became like
a child that is thwarted, and a froward child at
that. 'Twas the merest folly, for what did he
expect? What had he said himself he expected,
when Mr. Phillips offered himself at first to be
his envoy? 'Good my lord,' it now appeared
he looked the town should have said, as soon as
he was known to be at the gates, 'be pleased to
enter and to put your foot upon our neck.'
'Twas in another fashion the town received his
overtures, as any that knew the temper of the
citizens might have told him. Having gone so
far as to shut their gates in the face of his

troops, my lord was no such mighty magician as to charm them open with one wave of his flag of truce. The men of Derry were minded to make good what they had done, and sent him word to that effect.

I was nothing disquieted on Mr. Phillips' account, knowing him too good a friend to the Protestant interest to be hurt by the men of Derry. His letter to my lord ran that he was detained by force; but we knew how force might well be friendship in masquerade in such a time.

And now there was a great council held in my poor house, what was best to be done. Sure, I began to be in pain lest nothing should be done but talk, until it should be too late in the day for them to quit Cloncally. But at last there was a getting to horse, and a marshalling of the men that had been brought in from their flight, and some short time before the falling of the dusk my lord Earl took a courteous leave of us, by the title of allies, and rid away for Coleraine with all his gentlemen, followed by his rabble. It was a long and a weary march for them so late in the day, and at such a season of the year.

As for my lady, it was clean impossible that she should attempt it. I had no choice but to set my house at her disposal, which offer she

accepted with a very ill grace, though I know
'twas little worse than my own in making it.
Truly, I had little mind for her company; but
what could one do? Not to allow a woman
delicately nurtured to venture forth upon a
journey of fourteen miles, in the dusk of a
December evening, were she the veriest shrew
and vixen that ever breathed. And this was
the ninth of the month, besides, the very night
of the massacre.

My Lord Antrim had very much heartened
us in respect to that terror, both by his language
about it, and by the perfect unconcern he
showed in riding away from his lady upon the
very eve of it. None the less, the most vigilant
watch was kept in our house all night, and who,
think you, was the heart and soul of it? Who
but Captain Hamilton, who made his appearance
between five and six of the clock, as he had
done on the memorable Friday evening, but in
a far different frame of mind. This time it was
as a jest, a frolic, that he bade me regard his
coming.

'Sure, what did you expect?' asked he of
me. 'Did you think I'd stop in Derry, away
from you, at such a time? If you did, your
penetration was much at fault. I rid to Derry
with the best will in the world, 'tis true, finding
my quarters here something over-hot for com-

fort, with so many that knew me in the house. But be sure I had a plan in my mind ; I saw a way clear to return or ever I left, else had I never left.'

'And the plan ?' I asked him. We were safe in Roland's nursery, but yet I was all in a quaking, lest he had run into a trap. 'Do you know that my Lady Antrim and her confessor are still in the house, and her ladies ?'

'The plan ?' said he, ignoring the rest of my question. 'Why, 'twas the very self of simplicity. Having brought Mr. Phillips to the town-hall, I took leave to quit his service with the same absence of ceremony I'd assumed it with. I went straight to your father's house (where, by the way, I had an astonishingly good reception), changed my suit of livery for some of Wamphray's clothes, completed my beggar's errand by borrowing a boat, and rowed back here as fast as I could lay oars to water. I came reconnoitring up the brook, and was in time to see my lord Earl and his company taking their departure ; then, the coast being clear, I made my way, with Annot's help, into the house, by the back-door.'

'The coast clear indeed !' said I. 'Did you hear me tell you that my lady Countess is here still ?'

'Why, yes,' said he coolly ; 'somebody down-

stairs mentioned the same thing or ever I set
foot inside the house, I believe. I can't say I
was much impressed by it. Her ladyship does
not appear to me in the light of a probable captor,
whatever she may do to you.'

'She may be all as much to be feared ; she
or her priest might easily put others on your
track,' said I. 'You ran a nearer risk than you
knew to-day already.'

And thinking him far too much disposed to
make light of the risks he ran, I even told him
every word of the conversation I had overheard.
He laughed.

'Charmingly tricked, as a man could have
done it if he'd gone about to endeavour it!'
said he; 'I wish I knew their names. But
these I suppose you wouldn't tell me if you
knew them.'

He was right in that conjecture, and I told
him so.

'A woman,' quoth he, 'hath a poor idea
indeed of repaying a piece of friendship. But,
Lord, Mary! if you could but see the state the
town's in! Never was anything like it, save
a fermenting vat. They were on the very
brink of admitting the Red-shanks—the very
brink! The potent had been presented, and
was gone to the Mayor to be allowed; in
another minute they'd have been in possession,

and the city at their mercy. For none of the
headmen could make up their minds to take
the responsibility of disowning the King's
commission. But at that moment thirteen
brave 'prentice-boys were found to make up
theirs. They ran together and shut the gates
in the Red-shanks' faces—slammed them, by
Jove!—and balked the butchers of their prey.
The first step being taken, the magistrates
were nothing loath to follow; they found some
pretext, good enough to stand as a shield
betwixt their loyalty and their lives. And now
they're as thankful as—well, as they should be,
to these gallant 'prentices, whose names, sure,
will never perish while Derry's a city.'

He paid so much deference to my fears,
though he scoffed at them, as to keep well out
of sight of my Lady Antrim and her party,
which proved the easier that an escort came
for them early the next day from Coleraine.
Never in the world, I believe, was hostess
better pleased to see the last of guest than was
I, as my lady took her departure with her
gentlewomen, and her priest, and her pets,
and her petulance. And not a sound (for 'twas
the first word we asked them) had these
gentlemen heard, any more than ourselves, of
the terrible massacre. Neither sound nor sign
of it was there, they told us, between Coleraine

and Cloncally; the country lay as quiet and unmolested as though there were never an Ultogh within an hundred miles.

Was the terror, then, actually at an end? We put the question to each other as we returned into the house after their departure. 'Twas the hardest thing in the world to think so, and yet so it verily seemed. The day that was to have ended us, and cleared the province of English blood, by a very bloody method, was come and gone, and had left neither trace nor scath. Whether, as my Lord Antrim told us, the whole thing was from the first nothing but a malicious jest, designed to make a laughing-stock of the Protestants in the eyes of all Ireland; whether the famous Comber letter was written by a true man, but one that was himself deceived; or whether it was my Lord Antrim that was deceived, and there was a plot indeed, whereof he had no knowledge, but the resistance of Derry broke the neck of it, so that it came to naught, I know not; and none hath ever been able to discover. Much that passed in Ulster, both before and after the siege, conspires to give a colour of likelihood to the last supposition. But however it may have been, there was never more heard of the massacre, save in the way of recollection and speculation.

And now that the road to Derry lay as open
to us as we could wish, what hindered us to
take it? Why were we not up and away to
Derry and good neighbourhood as soon as my
Lady Antrim's coach was out of sight?

Faith, I ask myself the question, and can
scarce find any answer to it. For one thing,
there was no longer fear at our heels to drive
us; the immediate danger, whatever it had
been, was past. And that being the case, it
will be no surprise to any that hath ever
managed either a house or an estate, to learn
that there appeared an hundred things to do to
put the place in proper order to be left.

I little doubt, however, but that I and my
women had been despatched to Derry that
same day, in company of Mr. Browning, but
for a letter that came from Wamphray, giving
an account of all that had been done in the
town since the Friday, far more minute than
Captain Hamilton had been able to gather in
his hurried visit. After all the good and com-
fortable news came some that was a perfect
satire upon it—to wit, the sending of deputa-
tions to Dublin and to London to excuse the
conduct of the town in those quarters where
offence was like to be taken at it. 'Twas
enough to move our laughter.

'Why, now,' said Captain Hamilton, 'did I

tell you the reason why they fired those great
guns that frightened Antrim's men so horribly?
'Twas joy—a salute to Prince George of
Denmark for having left King James and gone
over to the Prince of Orange.'

'I can't wonder at them, for all that,' said
Mr. Browning, 'nor blame them, either; for
they can't be in a state to make any effectual
resistance to well-appointed troops, such as are
sure to be sent down against them. There
must be some at headquarters, to be sure, that
know what case they're in. They have no
choice but to make terms for the present,
though, to speak of them as they merit, I
believe there are no men in Ireland less fickle
or more steadfast than the men of Derry.
Waverers—half-hearted folk and indifferent—
what place is free of them? What cause hath
not some of them, to its curse? But the bulk
of the men of Derry are of another temper.'

'I think no less of them, indeed,' said Captain
Hamilton, 'and by consequence I believe
they've reason good enough for what they're
doing to-day, which, do you see, throws an
entirely new complexion on what *we* should
do. Mary, I mean, and yourselves. For
myself, it matters not one whit; there or here,
I'm marked for a rebel, and shall be treated
accordingly, if ever they lay hands on me,

which the Fates avert! But for her, being
by great good fortune, and by the merest
chance in the world, on the safe side of the
hedge, I'd be for having her stay there. Some
of these good folks in Derry would be well
enough pleased to be in her shoes, apparently.'

'Your proposal, then, I take it, is that she
should stay here till the town's affairs are composed,' said Mr. Browning.

'When he is with me,' I rejoined, 'I'd as
lief be here as anywhere else in the world.'

'I can't be with you very long, however,'
quoth Captain Hamilton gravely.

'Why not?' said I. 'Sure, you run no more
risk now in your own house than in the house
of any of your friends. All are in the same
case—known for favourers of the Prince of
Orange, and by consequence held traitors to
King James.'

He laughed.

'It's the last of my thoughts, or of any man's
that I care to call friend,' said he, 'to sit down
in any house, were it the strongest in Ireland,
and wait our fate. I must be up and away upon
my business in a very short time, I assure you.'

'And leave me here by myself?' said I.
'Never, surely! I would not pass another
week like the last for a thousand pound in my
hand.'

'Nor would I ask it of you, sweetheart; be assured of that,' said he. 'I mean you to delay only till this business be arranged and settled.'

I threw out my hands with something of passion in the gesture.

'See,' I said—and my voice was pitiful in mine own ears—'what a coil we be in! No side but hath its pitfall; no step to be taken but it may lead toward destruction. An hour ago I'd have been charmed to be sure of another fortnight here to set things orderly and safe before they be left—I'd have been just as pleased to be gone to Derry to safety and the company of friends—now I care not for either; each is a snare, and which the worst none but a seer can tell.'

Mrs. Browning took my hand in hers and fondled it out of mere pity. If a man's presence be protection in our troubles, sure 'tis a woman's that is comfort. I came so nigh to weeping that I lost some of the talk between her husband and mine. When next I took note of it they were speaking of that which Captain Hamilton had let drop — of riding abroad presently upon business of importance. He was giving Mr. Browning some account, though very guarded and careful, of the first beginnings of that confederacy of the Protestant

gentry in Ulster that came afterwards to be
called the Antrim Association, whereof he was
from the first a notable and leading member.

They say that 'tears dim the eye,' but that's
a fable; nor is there any more truth in the companion saying that 'grief dulls the heart to all
but itself.' 'Tis the clean contrary. Tears but
wash the eye to see the clearer, and grief doth
put the heart in touch with a thousand things
that else it had been dull to.

My heart and eyes being thus opened and
thus washed, there was discovered to them a
thing whereof till then I had never dreamed—
to wit, the alchemy of war; and how when a
man comes but to the verge of its fiery circle
his quality is tested as by nothing else on earth.
He that in time of peace stood as a rare good
fellow, an excellent companion over a bottle,
is now no more than a rotten stick, a mere
bag of wind; or else perhaps he is now no
more a pleasant companion, but a true and
trusty comrade. I sat silent on my chair, and
heard near every man of my acquaintance
weighed and classed, and it was like the parting of the sheep from the goats at the Day
of Judgment. Among the goats were many
ancient and beloved friends to all of us; they
spoke of such with all affection—nay, I thought
sometimes with affection and respect made but

the keener by their differences. Sure, it was
no light thing that set the hand of my husband
against the hand of such a man as Patrick
Sarsfield, or put him in opposition to so many
of his own kindred and name. A verse of
Holy Scripture came so forcibly into my head,
and so often, that at last I spoke it out.

'"A man's foes,"' said I, '"shall be they of
his own household."'

'Ay, truly,' said Mr. Browning. '"Brother
shall deliver up brother to death, and the parent
the child;" so it hath been always in such
times of heart-searching, and so it shall ever
be. There's no tie of kindred so strong but a
true conviction will break it.'

'But why,' exclaimed Captain Hamilton—
'why can't they open their eyes and look?
The truth here is as plain as the sun at noon;
'tis mere blindness that will deny it.'

'There was never any such truth from the
beginning of the world,' said Mr. Browning.
'Think of the old fable of the shield that was
golden on the one side and silver on the other.
Such a shield is every matter that can be so
much as questioned.'

'This cannot be questioned,' exclaimed Captain Hamilton, with conviction. 'Who can
doubt the duty of faithfulness to truth, and to
liberty of conscience?'

'Or who, say they,' replied the other, 'can call in question the duty of loyalty to the sovereign, Divinely anointed as he is? No, Hamilton; our side of the shield is the golden one, or so we think it; but theirs is as righteous in their own eyes, and perhaps is precious metal also.'

'Hang it, man!' said Captain Hamilton, 'you're talking like one of the waverers exactly. Take heed you be not found yourself among the half-hearted, when all's done.'

'That certainly were destruction,' said he, with a gleam on his face between meditation and smiling.

By some strange trick of the mind, that and his words together set my memory questing into the past; and the thing it brought to my recollection was the conversation we had upon the day after Captain Hamilton's escape. Then also he had shown a tolerance—nay, a fellow-feeling—for those of the opposite party that was wonderful in a man of opinions so strong. It threw me into a fit of musing, wherein word by word, picture by picture, came back into my mind the marvellous story he had told us, and its application. That which he had said, and for which my husband had blamed him, had something of the same spirit. Here again were men of different creeds contending ; for, sure, a man hath a creed in politics no less than in religion. Here again was one that acknowledged kindred in spirit in spite of difference in form. I marvelled at it, but in a groping fashion I understood.

For here, likewise, each was ' firmly persuaded in his own mind,' and reverenced in his adversary that which made his own virtue. Here again it was a kind of measure of the virtue, that it could accord reverence to that which was so opposite to itself.

Yes, mine eyes were opened, and I saw the beauty of the saying as I had not done at first. Blind mortals as we be, and so easily led astray, 'tis ' for the truth ' we should strive rather than against the error. Being well-nigh as like to err as to breathe, as we are, is it the less our duty to uphold to our last gasp the truth we be persuaded of ? Is it not, indeed, the source and summit of any worthiness we have ?

And if it be, how dare we refuse to others, our fellows, a like duty and right ? It came again to the old conclusion—the chivalrous conclusion that hath braced the arm of so many a champion from old time till now—Let each do his devoir knightly and worthily, and may God show the right.

My mind dropped down from these aerial

flights, and mine eyes along with it ; and then
I was suddenly aware that all this while they
had been fixed full, but unseeing, on Mr.
Browning's. With most men that had put me
to the blush ; but with him it mattered not a
whit. By some strange inner vision I divined
in him a similar train of thought to my own.

'" *Ô sanctâ simplicitas*," ' said I, as our eyes
met.

''Tis the whole case in a nutshell,' he rejoined.

Captain Hamilton looked as though he
thought us suddenly gone demented.

' If that's your way of discussing your preparations for getting you gone to Derry,' said
he, ' then I've forgot my Latin.'

I laughed in my own despite.

' I can make no plans for that to-day,' said I ;
' I have no heart for it. To-morrow—wait
till to-morrow. To-morrow I'll set about it in
earnest, both plans and preparations. I cannot choose but think of all that is past so newly
to-night. To-morrow I'll wake with mine eyes
turned towards the future.'

CHAPTER XVII.

HOW ONE OF US REFUSED TO QUIT CLONCALLY.

ON the morrow, therefore, we began to prepare for leaving Cloncally; 'twas a heavy task for the few hands that remained to execute it, and made the heavier by the ill-liking we had to it. But 'needs must,' if it hath no law, neither doth it brook paltering; and it was needs must now with us.

Had the choice of a boon been offered me in these days, I make little doubt but I had asked for a glimpse into the near future; 'twas a thing I could not hinder myself from musing upon day and night. What did I think to see, I wonder, that I longed so greatly to lift the veil which hid it? Did I think myself upon another Mount of Pisgah, whence another Land of Promise was to be descried? Perhaps I was, had I been endowed with the prophet's full gift of vision. But across what burning deserts of trial, across what rivers of bitterness, across what a Red Sea of blood and death, had I discerned its beauties! And all these were to be traversed, though scarce a soul of us guessed the least of them, ere that good land and large, where we be now arrived, should be won.

Among all our causes innumerable for gratitude to the Father of mercies, is there any, I wonder, greater than this, that in His dealings with us purblind mortals He doth guide Himself by His own knowledge and not by our prayers?

As to the preparations that busied us, both for our subsistence during our sojourn in Derry and for the safe-keeping of that part of our property that could not be taken with us (for lack of fodder or of storage-room), 'twere both tedious and useless to record them. To what purpose should I set down the names of those who had charge of the young cattle, or of those that were entrusted with the milch kine; to what places of supposed security they were taken by those faithful servants, and how bestowed to escape the eyes of those hungry foragers that it needed no gift of prophecy to expect? That a great contribution, both in cattle and grain, was despatched to Derry towards the maintenance of the troops there, 'tis likewise unnecessary for me to mention; for what man was there among the Protestant gentry of the province that did not the same, according to his means and quality? He that had money gave money; he that had men brought these; he that had store of provision sent that; some that had none of such things gave others that were as valuable, as Mr. Morrison and Mr. Sherman, the apothecaries, of their drugs, and Harvey and Curlew their time and trouble in administering the stores that were sent in.

Every day, by some sure messenger, we had tidings from the city, and it was nothing less than wonderful how all was organized there. All the men in the place that were fit to bear arms were by this time formed into six companies, and kept watch and ward turn and turn about, for all the world like professed soldiers. And every householder had his time appointed to hang out lighted cressets on his house-front, so that the city was conveniently lighted by night, and the business of its defence went on near as well as by day.

All this was done systematically, though it was well enough known that envoys were gone both to Tyrconnel and to London to excuse the behaviour of the city to the Red-shank garrison. It was said with praise that, however our chiefs might hope for a fair answer, they would be ready for a rough one. Another thing that was both observed and commended was the ad-

vancing of five out of the thirteen 'prentice-boys
(that had been foremost in the affair of the
shutting of the gates) to be officers of the city
guard; three of them being appointed ensigns,
and two lieutenants. The head-men of Derry
had evidently no intention of disowning them
that under God had been the salvation of the
place.

I presently found that, in spite of the dis-
taste I had to life in the city, much of mine
interest and most of my thoughts were gone
thither in advance of me. But there be two
things of those that happened before we quitted
our own pleasant home that have places in this
narrative, and cannot be omitted from it.

The first is the unaccountable conduct of
Andrew Wilson, the gardener, which angered
me not a little at the time, though in after-days
it turned so greatly to mine aid. He was the
same man that, upon the terrible evening of the
7th, had quitted his post in the front of the
house to listen to the parleying that was going
on in the rear thereof. Certes, after the reproof
he then received, and the way he took it, I had
thought Andrew bound to me and to my service
as much as Annot his wife—next to Margery
Hamilton, the most faithful of all my women.

But now there appeared reason to doubt
whether this were so indeed; for the man

began to show a pernicious habit of being absent
from his post again and again. 'Tis true, that
whatever was given him to do he did; even
creditably and punctiliously. But the thing
being done, where was Andrew? Nowhere to
be seen; though, to be sure, he came when
called, and that without any great delay.

After a few days this began to annoy me
mightily. It was not, indeed, that his absences
caused much inconvenience; but, then, they
were unaccountable, and consequently provok-
ing. Why in the morning, when the other men
came to take their orders, was Andrew never
with them till he was sent for? Why at dinner-
time did he constantly make his appearance
when the rest had half finished? Why, if at
any chance moment during the day he was
needed, was it always necessary to send for
him? And why was he still so eager to be
gone the moment he could be spared? In
former times he had been the exact contrary of
all this. Not dilatory, perhaps, considering his
age, but leisurely in all he did. An excellent
trencherman, and in no hurry to set it by.
Above all, a gossip in grain—willing to suspend
any occupation to discuss the smallest piece of
news with anybody, pleased especially if his
betters should notice him or converse with him.

The thing was a mystery to me, and as such

to be solved. But sure there was so much to
see to, that it was not till he had been out of the
way when wanted that I questioned him. I
spoke, I hope, with great mildness; for, being
an old and trusted servant of the family, he was
neither to be harshly treated nor lightly accused.
Nevertheless, he cast a very angry glance toward
the kitchen, whence came the sound of women's
voices—Margery's, to wit, and that of Annot
his wife.

'Hoots, my leddy!' said he, 'ye wadna heed
a blash o' clash—idle clavers!'

This, however, was scarce the answer to
satisfy me.

'You forget,' said I to him in a tone of voice
something sterner, 'that I have eyes and ears
of my own. No one hath brought me evil
reports of you. I have seen for myself that
you're never at hand of late—never to be found
without search. What's the meaning of it?'

'I was never far to seek,' returned he. 'I'm
gey an' sure naebody's ever needed to cry on
me twice.'

This was true, and though it seemed designed
to put me in the wrong, I at once admitted it.

'But,' said I to him, 'why should you be to
seek at all? You were never wont to be so.'

The old man turned upon me like a dog that
snarls at the whip.

'Weel, my leddy,' said he, 'was I ever to seek when there was aucht set me to do, or hae ye ony fau't to find wi' onything ye ever gae me to do ?'

'No, never,' I replied ; and was about to add what, when all's said, is the truth, that 'tis part of the duty of every mistress to know where to find any of her servants at any moment ; but he broke out angrily :

'Aweel, then, I think ye hae little to do to find fau't wi' me. Feggs! them 'at couldna find me was gey slack seekers. A whistle frae your fine siller ca' wad hae brocht me in a meenit.'

With that he turned and left my presence, not waiting my dismissal. I for my part stood astonished. The man had now and then permitted himself small liberties of speech with his master and myself, such as were very pardonable in so old a servant ; but never before had he transgressed the bounds of strict respect.

Now that he had done so so completely, I was a little put to it to know what order to take with him. To speak to him again, and be met most likely with sullenness, were a course wanting in dignity ; while, on the other hand, should I mention the matter to Captain Hamilton, he was sure to be over-harsh with the old man. For now I made sure that there was some

trouble in his mind that had caused him to
speak to me in so unwonted a manner. I fell
to wondering what this secret trouble might be,
but could imagine no explanation that was either
likely or sufficient.

He went about all the rest of that day in a
very hang-dog fashion; and certainly there was
no need to send for him, he seemed to be trying
to catch my eye wheresoever I turned. Not
having decided what to do, I looked not near
him; and when I had aught to say to him, I
made Cargill my spokesman. Perhaps this was
enough to show him his fault, or perhaps his
own conscience did that without hint from me.
At any rate, he lay in wait for me towards
evening, and accosted me.

'Madam,' said he, 'I was sair to blame to
speak back till ye as I did, and I crave your
pardon.'

'You were,' said I. 'I was astonished, and
very angry with you.'

'Nae doot, nae doot,' said he with contrition.
'But them 'at seeks a man suld seek him in his
ain bit. Had I bin socht in ma gairden, fac',
I'd 'a bin fund.'

This explanation was as singular as his behaviour; for what hath a gardener to do in his
garden in the month of December? Andrew
was known for a man of probity, or else I had

begun to suspect him shrewdly of a design to throw *dust in mine eyes*, as the saying hath it. The more I turned it about the less I made of it, and therefore the next morning I even put the matter to the test.

'Come, Andrew Wilson,' said I to him, ' show me this great piece of work that hath taken up every spare minute you've had for a week past.'

I went towards the garden, and he followed me thither without a word.

At the first glance all seemed there as it ever doth in the winter—that is to say, blank spaces beset with dead bushes, and separated by alleys of grass which stood rank and rimy. But down the middle of the midmost path there was a track, whereon the grass was trodden flat and the hoar-frost gone. This track we followed, and in the middle of the garden, where the wide alley crosses it from side to side, we came to a new-set hedge of quicks, the bushes so high and thick that it must have been a heavy task to transplant them ; not to mention the still greater labour of bringing them from the wood that bounds one side of the garden, and through which the brook descends, in leaps and rapids and quiet pools, to join the river.

Andrew looked upon the hedge with a kind of gloomy satisfaction.

' It's a gran' season for transplantin',' quoth

he meditatively. 'A wee stiff to steer wi' the frost in the gr'und, but no a drap o' sap startin'; a' dead sleepin'. Come May, noo, or maybe come April, there's no a crater, unless he's bin bred a gaird'ner, will ever think that hedge a day less than ten year auld.'

'Perhaps not,' said I. 'But what's the use of it?' And perhaps I put the question sharply, for the hedge was an ugly blemish in my fair garden.

He looked at me with commiseration for my ignorance.

'What use, my leddy?' quoth he, with a pitying smile. 'It's weel seen ye hae nae mind o' the Forty-ane.'

So it might be thought, considering that I was not born for more than twenty years after that! I laughed as he said it.

'I was a hafflins laddie at the time,' quoth Andrew. 'But, losh, I mind it yet! My certie, if ye had but seen the gairdens thae sogers left ahint them, ye wadna be speerin the use o' a hedge! A herd o' swine, an' every sow wi' a deevil in its belly, couldna hae wrocht mair mischeef.'

Still I did not see—and so I told him—what his hedge should do in the way of restraining such riotous creatures.

'If it were to keep them out of the garden,'

said I, ' I'd understand it; but here's more than half of it left undefended and open, before ever you come at the hedge.'

' Aha! my lady,' quoth he triumphantly; ' they may even tak' their wull o' *this* hauf o't. Ere I quit Cloncally, a'thing worth castin' a thocht till will be planted on the tither side o' that hedge. A' my Virginia strawberries is there already.'

' But what's to keep them from breaking through as soon as they see that the better part of the garden's on the other side of the hedge ?' I asked him.

' Ou, but ye see that's juist what they'll *no* see,' quoth Andrew. ' The hedge is gey an' heigh e'en noo; an' 'twill be gey an' thick as weel, come simmer. It a' lies in sae weel, too ; the slope o' the gr'und fits in sae bonnily. Wad ye no think yoursel', ma leddy, 'at the gairden ended there, if so be ye didna ken better ?'

' I think I'd try to peep over it, all the same,' said I ; ' and so, take my word for it, will the Irish soldiers—if they come.'

' Ou, they'll maybe *no* come,' he admitted. ' Ye hae a chance. Cloncally's no on nane o' the main roads, an' no sae terrible near the ceety, neither. You'll maybe be passed over ; I'll no say. But gin they come, let them peep, for An'ra. I hae a plan o' stickin' in a bit sauch-

buss here, an' a bit sauch-buss there ; an' by the
time the leaf be green, I'll wad my best pair o'
breeks there's naebody 'll ever jalouse it's ony
mair nor a waste bit.   They'll be gey daft that'll
push through a quick-thorn hedge to win at the
like o' that.'

It seemed no better than trifling to me to
provide with such sedulous care for the preserva-
tion of a few shrubs and herbs, when so many
things of far more value, and more like to take
harm, must even be left to their fate.   But who
could find it in his heart to say as much to a
man whose soul was so wrapped up in his work
as Andrew's ?   I was turning back to the
house, with even a word of encouragement on
my lips, when he led me to the right, along the
wide green alley.

'For ye may as weel see the haill o't, since
ye're here,' he reflected aloud.

The rest of it was a plan he had for de-
stroying the wilderness, that is the lowest
part of the garden, beyond the little summer-
house, in the same manner, by filling it with
sallows and other things that take root easily
and grow fast, so as to make of it a thicket that
should seem as it had never been touched by
the hand of man.   Then the part of the garden
which held his cherished plants would be converted into a kind of island—a place cut off on

all sides from intrusion, or even suspicion.
Had the end been but worth the pains, it had
been a clever plan enough.

But complete as he had made it, he seemed
unsatisfied, and mused and murmured as he was
leading me back to the house.

'I'm terrible vexed at leavin' thae Virginia
strawberries,' said he. 'A' the way frae
Hamilton, in Scotland, I got them; I'd 'a likit
weel to see hoo they turned oot. The Duke's
gaird'ner tellt me there never was sic fruit seen
in this country.'

He seemed still to muse with discontent upon
the prospect of leaving them, even after the
pain he had been at to conceal them. As I was
going into the house he stopped me, laying his
hand upon mine arm.

'Feggs!' said he. 'I've gude a-mind to
bide here, an' tak' my chances, as weel as my
gairden.'

This was the first time, evidently, that the
idea had entered his head; but having once
thought of it, he grew every day more in love
with the notion. The man's whole heart was
in his work, as I said but a moment ago, and
any hardship that he might suffer by staying at
Cloncally seemed ever the slighter, the more he
thought of it, in comparison with the grief of
leaving his plants bereft of his fostering care.

He turned the project over and over in his mind, until it grew into a resolution, and then he announced it.

'Them 'at likes can gang intil Derry,' said he; 'but it's nane o' An'ra. *A*'ll bide whaur I am.'

To this he stuck, in spite of all expostulations. Whatever we might urge of the dangers he ran by remaining, he answered us after that in one set formula, which was this:

'Weel, weel, I'm gaun nae sic airt; no a fit o' me!'

And once, when Annot, his wife, importuned him to change his mind, he so far departed from his Puritan sobriety of phrase as to express it thus: '*De'il* a fit o' An'ra; de'il a fit o' me! I've said it, and I'll stick til't.'

After that we knew that his resolve was indeed taken, and forbore to urge him any more to change it.

CHAPTER XVIII.

HOW THE LORD VISCOUNT MOUNTJOY CAME BACK TO CLONCALLY.

AND now the intelligence that reached us daily from the city (for, naturally, there was a constant coming and going between Cloncally and the house we were going to, and every man that went in upon an errand brought back a return cargo of tidings) began to be all of the approach of my Lord Mountjoy. All the talk, likewise, was of the articles that should be agreed to between him and the city.

There was a mighty discomfortable rumour in the air that he was sent down by the Lord Deputy with the full strength of his regiment, to reduce the place ; 'twas much debated, but little heeded, if I may set down a statement that hath so much the look of a contradiction. Contradiction there is none in reality, for though it was very likely that Tyrconnel had given charge to my lord to be sharp and severe with us, yet

he was known for one that would be just, at all
hazards. And from strict justice, the men of
Derry thought themselves to have little to
fear.

I have sometimes heard the Lord Deputy
Tyrconnel described as a great administrator,
and that by persons who should, as I thought,
have known better. Such an estimate doth
argue partiality rather than judgment, to my
mind. Violence is not strength, neither is deceit
ability; and if a man be known for one that
speaks ever fairer than he means, save when he
threatens more than he dares, what value do
men put upon his promises, or what fear do
they attach to his threats?

That was my Lord Deputy Tyrconnel—
violent to mere brutality when there was no
reprisal to be apprehended; apt to menace
those he dared not lift a finger against; ready
to promise anything in the world to gain an
end, but never casting a thought to the performance of his promise when the end was
gained, unless, indeed, he had in view some
other remoter purpose. But tyrannous, false,
unscrupulous as he was, he had a good thought
and a true insight when he determined to send
my Lord Mountjoy into the North to deal with
Derry.

My lord was a Royalist, and yet an ardent

Protestant, accredited, therefore, as one might say, to both sides, and acceptable to the moderate men of both ; one that was known to be as faithful to his undertakings as the Lord Deputy was faithless ; loyal to his friends, and just to such as differed from him ; he was the picked man for the work, and Tyrconnel, for once, had the wit to see it.

And yet I have sometimes wondered, in the light of his after-conduct, whether 'twas my lord Viscount's personal fitness that had weight with him, or another accidental advantage which he possessed—to wit, his office of Master of the Ordnance in the kingdom. This placed him, as it were, *behind the scenes* with us, so that he knew, and must have informed my Lord Deputy, of that which was the weak point of our whole position ; which was (as Mr. Browning had surmised at the first rumour of their endeavour to justify themselves with the authorities) the lack of arms and ammunition. It was common talk by this time, that there were but one or two barrels of powder in the magazine ; and this, of course, the Lord Mountjoy was as well aware of as they that had the charge of it. Add to this knowledge of his, of their weakness, the confidence and respect they had in his character and for his person, and it should seem as though there were little

needed to induce or else to compel their submission.

There was no house in the province, I believe, where the state of affairs was oftener or
more keenly debated than in ours. Captain
Hamilton, who long ere this had cast aside his
disguise, and was riding hither and thither
openly in his own name, among men that were
as deeply dipped as himself, had it continually
on his lips. The views of near every man of
weight in Derry were known to him, and were
such as he approved.

'By mine honour!' he would say, 'if Mountjoy looks that they should lay their neck under
his heel, he'll be finely astonished, that's all!
The men that have drawn the sword are ready
to abide its award, rather than betray a hair of
the meanest head in the city to punishment—
ay, even they that were the most anxious to
clear themselves in Tyrconnel's eyes. It's not
Mountjoy's advantage in the power of powder
and shot that'll bring them to their knees, and
so he'll find, however little he likes it!'

Never yet, as he showed each time he heard
or mentioned the name of Lord Mountjoy, had
Captain Hamilton forgiven him for what he
deemed his unfair dealing towards himself.
And I, that could have shown him how far the
lord Viscount's intentions had been from un-

friendship towards him, had perforce to hold
my tongue, being bound in respect of that
unruly member by my lord's saying ' that he
committed his honour into my keeping.'

Presently we had certain news, no less than
by an envoy sent into Derry in the person of
Captain MacAusland, that Lord Mountjoy was
come as near to us as to Omagh. Next he was
come as far as to Raphoe, and some of the
head-men of the city were gone to confer with
him there, and to endeavour to agree upon
articles.   In that, it presently appeared, they
were unsuccessful ; for my lord was come as
near as to Strabane, where he was to receive
another set of deputies from Derry ; but of that
which was agreed to between them, or whether
any articles at all had been agreed to, we could
get no certain information, and each fresh report
was a flat contradiction of the last.   The fact
was that the citizens themselves had no better
grounds than guesses and surmises for their
reports.   This alone was certainly known : that
the terms the city stood out for were such, both
for safety and for honour, that my lord Viscount
had either no mind or no power to grant them.

This was the state of matters, one dark and
drizzling day, at the darkest of the year, when
I was alone in the house, save for the servants,
Captain Hamilton having ridden abroad upon

his business. We were but awaiting the settlement between my lord and the city to begone from Cloncally; and to say the truth, Cloncally was so far dismantled that 'twas no longer a very enticing abode to linger in. I passed from room to room, noting the bareness of each and the coldness; the sound of the rain upon the windows brought it to a point of very wretchedness. I was well-nigh reconciled to be gone, and every gust of the raw, chilling wind seemed to set my heart the looser from the ties of home.

Presently Cargill came in search of me, with a face full of hesitation and doubt.

'An it please you, madam,' said he, 'there's a party of gentlemen below desiring to see you. It's no day to keep them cooling themselves at the door until I make sure of your pleasure, and so I have even shown them in to the hall-fire.'

'Why, that was very right of you,' said I. 'Why do you look strangely at me? sure, any that come to Cloncally on such a day must be friends indeed—or else foes indeed, and be here upon pressing business.'

'Why, that's the reason,' said Cargill. 'Matters went none so smoothly the last time they were at Cloncally. I scarce knew whether to ask them in, or to shut the door in their faces.'

'Who are they?' said I.

'My Lord Mountjoy is one,' said Cargill, and was about to name the others, but I cut him short.

'My Lord Mountjoy!' I said; 'and you're in doubt whether to let him in or no!' Then remembering that he knew no more than the surface, so to speak, of my lord's behaviour to his master, 'Cargill,' said I, 'you've heard of the folly of *quarrelling with one's bread and butter*, no doubt? Take my word for it, 'tis no wiser to quarrel with one that holds our fortunes —and perhaps our lives—in his hand! Go quickly to my lord, and show him all becoming courtesy; I'll be with him in a minute.'

'And what of the master and his pleasure?' said the old man, still with a very dubious face. 'And his safety even, for aught I know?'

'You will cause one of the men to await him at the turn of the road,' said I. 'Let him know who is in the house, and he will do what he thinks fit.'

But, in truth, I had little fear for his safety. My lord had no doubt given me warning that, should he find him again in his power, he should have no choice but to take him. But that, though but three weeks ago in time, was *an age ago*, in all reason. Since then, the whole Protestant gentry of the North had got themselves as deeply tinctured with rebellion as he;

and my lord Viscount would find his hands
something over-full were he to attempt to take
every man that had made himself obnoxious to
the representatives of King James.

All this time I knew nothing of the names of
the Lord Mountjoy's companions. My astonishment was not small to find that one of them was
no other than Colonel Lundy, whom I had little
cause to love. The other was my lord's young
son Marmaduke. So chilled to the bone he
seemed, that I disguised my surprise at seeing
Lundy by making some little bustle about the
lad's comfort. He saw it, nevertheless—no
doubt his conscience made him clear of sight—
and taxed me with it.

'I believe,' said he, 'I'm the last man in the
regiment that you hoped to see in my lord's
company.'

'I had no reason,' said I coldly, 'to expect
the honour of a visit from my lord at all. Any
gentleman he brings with him must, of course,
share in his welcome.'

'However unwillingly?' said he, with an
odd kind of smile. 'Never trouble to deny
it, Mrs. Hamilton; I know you do not love
me.'

Whatever the man's motive was in forcing
me on so disagreeable an avowal, 'twould have
been out in another minute; for, sure, I had

never wrested my conscience to spare his feelings, and a half-denial in such a case is a whole confession.   But my lord interposed.

'I make little doubt,' said he, 'but you think we had neither of us much right to present ourselves in your house after what happened the last time we were here.   But I could not, somehow—perhaps I ought to have obtained your permission first—endure to be so near you and not to ask for myself how things have gone with you since that event; which, I'm sure you'll believe, I deplored the necessity of as much as yourself, or near it.   It hath been but an ill time since then for a lady to keep house by herself, unprotected.   Hath anyone molested you on account of Hamilton's imprudence?   I must take leave to tell you that I've suffered some anxiety lest they should.'

'So little,' said I, 'that it hath never once entered my head to think that such a thing was likely.'

'Now, that was strange,' said Lundy—'exceeding strange!   So unwonted an immunity might have set some minds speculating on the probability of *friends at Court.*'

He gave a very meaning glance towards my lord as he spoke.   But I endeavoured to look as though the glance were utterly lost on me, needing no warning to be careful in such a presence how I gave the least clue to any secret understanding between my lord and me.

'And if it be so,' I rejoined, 'my ignorance of the peril I stood in is no bar to my gratitude to any that hath interested himself in my behalf.'

'And if it were so,' said my lord, 'sure, there's little cause for gratitude, or for conceal- ment either, if a man have spoken a good word for the wife of a comrade of his that is under a cloud.'

This was so near an open avowal from the Lord Mountjoy of the pains he had been at to save me from punishment of some sort—per- haps from confiscation, perhaps from imprison- ment, possibly from both—that I could not forbear to thank him then and there. 'Twere an ill return to involve him in danger, no doubt, but it flashed across my mind that this could scarce be so wrested as to do him harm, his action in my favour being bound to be known to them he had approached on my behalf.

'Ah, my Lord Mountjoy,' said I to him, ''tis all very well to disclaim gratitude ; but, sure, he that renders another so great a service must even make up his mind to accept it. My insensibility to my danger doth only add strength to mine, now that my eyes are opened.' Words failed me to express my thanks, so that

I stretched out my hand to Lord Mountjoy, who took it and bent over it. 'You, too, Colonel Lundy,' said I, 'must accept my thanks, for that you opened mine eyes in mine own despite.'

'By the Lord! a scene of sentiment!' said a voice at the door of the room, so altered by surprise and resentment that I scarce knew it for my husband's.

He advanced into the room, bowing twice, almost to the ground, to my Lord Mountjoy. The lad, Marmaduke Stewart, on the settle by the fire, where I had placed him, gazed from one to another of us with wide-open, wondering eyes. Captain Hamilton bowed to him also with the most extreme ceremony.

'My lord Viscount!' said he. 'This is indeed a most unexpected visit, and one of which I feel myself totally unworthy. Your lordship's son, too! You do my poor house even too much honour. I own I was unprepared for it. God give me grace to show my gratitude!'

My lord had never a word to say, but stood as disconcerted as if he had really served Captain Hamilton the scurvy trick he believed. Only he stole a side-glance at me, as though he said, 'You can put this right, if it please you.'

For me, I had it on the tip of my tongue to explain. But, as if to bring me in mind of my clear duty, Captain Hamilton turned round to Lundy with hand outstretched, and voice that rang welcome—so to point the difference of his regard.

'Lundy!' said he. 'Dear old friend! This is a true pleasure; for I'm sure that you haven't come single-handed to catch me, for all as pernicious a rebel as some have done me the honour to make me out.'

For Lundy, he seemed to change in the twinkling of an eye, from the cold, sarcastic being he had been but the instant before my husband's appearance, to the bluff comrade, a little concerned to think what part he had played the last time his friend and he had been in company.

'Faith, Hamilton,' said he, 'there's not many would bear as little rancour as you do, considering how I was forced to treat you the last time I was in your house. You do me the justice to believe that 'twas nothing but a sense of duty that wrought with me—that's the truth. 'Tis no more than justice; but yet I thank you.'

The man's voice rang honesty so feelingly, that, faith, I went near to chide myself for my mistrust of him. On my husband the effect was different. I believe that, in his resentment against my lord, he had forgotten how keen Lundy had been to secure him; how unfriendly

he had behaved, and how set upon his undoing.
Of a sudden he remembered it, and he looked
upon Lundy strangely. Then again he held
out his hand to him.

'It's a fact,' said he, 'that you were something harsh with me that night, Lundy. Still,
perhaps you conceived yourself bound, as you
say. Let bygones be bygones, say I, and here's
my hand on it.'

It was like a reconciliation of two lovers.
Anyone had said that Lundy was affected nigh
to weeping. And yet, somehow, my distrust of
the man came uppermost once more.

Marmaduke Stewart behind me whispered his
father.

'Why does Hamilton flout you so?' said he.
'Why do you let him?'

'I have thrust myself into his house unbidden,'
said his father, very low, 'and must endure it.'

That recalled me to my senses. I took my
lord by the hand, and I rallied all my courage—
for, indeed, 'tis no pleasure to me, nor no light
thing, to brave my husband.

'That's excellently well said of you, my dear
James!' said I, striving to speak easily and
lightly, but only succeeding in speaking with a
quivering thickness in my voice—'excellently
well said! And it may apply to other cases
than Colonel Lundy's. Had you heard as you

came in what it was that my lord avowed—that
Colonel Lundy made him avow—of the friendship he hath showed me at Tyrconnel's court,
in preventing me from being molested on account
of your disgrace, or of what I did myself to get
you off, you'd be well assured that it was in
spite of a very real friendship for both of us
that he acted as he did. Let bygones be bygones say I as well as you, and please your
wife by being reconciled to one that I am sure
is your friend at heart.'

I reached my hand for his as I ceased speaking, meaning to have clasped it in Lord Mountjoy's; but Captain Hamilton hesitated.

'Befriended you?' said he. 'Why, I'm grateful for that! And I well believe there was
plenty of opportunity. Why, yes! now that I
think of it, there must have been somebody—
and somebody high in favour and influence—at
Tyrconnel's ear, else had you certainly heard
more of that night's work than you've done.
And yet he that sets the ball a-rolling may
very well try to guide it away from the innocent; 'tis no more than his duty.'

'Tis no more than his duty, indeed,' said
my lord very proudly. 'And Mrs. Hamilton
will do me the justice to bear me witness that I
claimed no thanks.'

At that Captain Hamilton caught him not by

one hand, but by both, shutting the left so hard upon my right hand that I winced; but sure, the pleasure of reconciling these two put the pain clean out of my head.

'Mountjoy,' said he, 'I've wronged you. I know it, and I ask your pardon. An old comrade, one that stood my friend always, I should have understood you better! You acted as you did for my sake; you meant to give me a chance, and you did.'

'Your wife,' said the other, with shining eyes —'your wife knew that from the first.'

Then, I promise you, my crushed hand pained me, and so did my heart. Here was a fine reward to my lord for his friendship, that the very thing I was bound by my promise to keep sacredly secret should come to light in the hearing of the man I most distrusted. He stepped forward with the most open brow in the world.

'That's as it should be, now,' said he. ''I make you my compliment, Mrs. Hamilton, on your talents as a peacemaker.'

So frank was he in his manner, and so much sincerity rang in his voice, that I could not choose but ask myself, 'Have I been all this time mistaken in the man?' Was this mere cowardice, I wonder, under the mask of charity? —a weak desire to shut mine eyes to the thing

that had been done, if Lundy were the traitor I
had hitherto thought him? That was what I
feared at first; but before we parted company
I was to find my doubts of him well-nigh lulled
to rest.

As for my lord, it was as though he had cast
a mask from his face and a weight from his
spirits; he became as gay as a schoolboy.
Captain Hamilton met him half-way; it was as
if the differences of their opinions were blotted
out and forgotten; they spoke with as little
appearance of reserve as though they were both
of a side. When I begged my lord's pardon for
serving him so far beneath his quality, for not
an ounce of plate was there left in the house to
set before him, 'Methinks,' said he, 'I see a
tablecloth; and that is so great and unwonted a luxury that it is impossible to take
note whether the dinner be served in plate or
in pewter.'

'You were never wont to be so Spartan in
your camp furniture,' said Captain Hamilton.

'No more I was,' he returned; 'but formerly
I was a man and a colonel of infantry. Now
I'm no better than a cannon-ball, fired by Tyrconnel at the head of your infant rebellion in
Derry. What time hath a cannon-ball to think
of comfort? I, upon my word, have had scarce
longer.' And so fell to describing the shifts he

had been put to on his march from Dublin, so
merrily that the hall rang with our laughter.

'It must be confessed you are reasonable
folks here in the North,' said he, when presently the talk had glanced round from his
march to his mission. 'You're aware, of course,
that I was written to—in the name of the city,
no less—to intercede with the Lord Deputy in
their behalf. I do so to the best of my poor
ability; and now that I am come in person to
accommodate matters, what do I find? Why,
that 'tis your very humble servant I am made,
to listen to your orders, not to make terms
between you and the authorities. Oh, it's the
plain fact!' he continued, as Captain Hamilton
seemed to demur. 'Phillips, Kennedy, and the
rest—you should hear them! "You will be
pleased," they tell me, "to get a general pardon
for us all." "Command me, by all means,"
I rejoin; "'tis no more than reason." "And
confirmed under the Great Seal," they proceed.
"Why, the Great Seal," I answer them, "is a thing
which I do not keep in my pocket; but I'll do
my best to fulfil your requirements!" "Until
you do," say they, "not a foot shall you set
inside our gates. You may even march back
by the way you came, and take your troops
with you."'

'Why, then,' said Captain Hamilton, 'I don't

desire to say a word to offend you ; but they've acted exactly as I expected, and I think you'll admit, Mountjoy, that they've acted like men. Haven't they, now ?'

'Like masters, rather,' said he.   ''Tis we that must act like men—eh, Lundy ?   I offered for their consideration—with the deepest respect, I assure you, not to say diffidence—that there's another to satisfy—the Lord Deputy, to wit.   "He might perhaps be so unreasonable as to look for a prisoner or two at my hands," said I.   " Say a 'prentice-boy or so, and one or two inconsiderable persons that were at the breaking-out of the riot."   " He may whistle for them," said they.   " Neither 'prentice nor pavior, nor any the most inconsiderable person in the city, shall he get, though he should ask for them upon his bended knees." '

''Tis very right of them to say so,' said Lundy.   'Sure, you would never expect them to disown them that were the saving of the city.'

Never before had I heard Lundy speak out fairly, either on the one side or the other.   I gazed at him, astonished both at his plainness and at the part he took, and, I promise you, I was not alone in my surprise.   My lord broke out laughing.

. . 'It spreads, I perceive,' said he.   'Lundy on

the side of rebellion! 'Tis Saul among the
prophets over again, only with a difference.
Then, no doubt,' said he, addressing Lundy,
'you approved their conduct to myself at their
gates this morning?'

'What was that, I pray you?' I put in, for of
this we had heard nothing.

'Why, a trifle!' said he, laughing —'the
merest trifle! The whole point of it lies in
the fact that 'twas my assistance they professed
to desire, and my intercession with the Lord
Deputy to arrange their affairs for them.
Faith, the man that intends to arrange the
affairs of Derry hath need of good gloves;
he'll come by the redding-stroke, or I'll never
earn my bread in the trade of a prophet. Why,
all they did to me, madam, was to treat me as
Antrim's proper successor. But bear in mind
that they besought me to assume the office.
They shut the gates in his face, and they would
not open them to me ; that's all. "Stay there,
good my lord," said they, "until you promise to
give us our own will in all things and singular
that have been brought in question." '

Captain Hamilton in his turn broke out a-
laughing.

'Is it even so, Mountjoy?' said he. 'Are
you no better than another captain of Red-
shanks, and are you come to Cloncally for sheer

lack of food and shelter? How if you had
found the birds flown and the nest cold?'

'Nay,' said my lord, 'in that case I had
merely been forced to ride back again and
claim them in Derry; for you shall understand
that they did open to me at last, "out of the
respect which they bear to my person," as they
say. But I shall have to give way to them at
last, I am assured; that grows the plainer at
every conference. And this is what they are
pleased to call "making an accommodation"!
I protest I never was so lessoned since my
governor ceased to bear rule over me when I
was a lad.'

Lundy looked from one to another of us, as
though about to take a plunge into unknown
waters.

'Can you blame them, my lord,' said he
slowly, 'considering what they are accused of,
and the man they are to deal with behind yourself? I can't; I confess it.'

'Well, I can't,' said Lord Mountjoy, grown
suddenly serious. ''Tis very fact that King
James's subjects have need of every safeguard
they can procure from his representatives when
they stand accused of high treason and rebellion.'

'King James's subjects!' said Colonel Lundy,
with an intonation of reflection. 'I wonder

how long they will continue in that relation to him.'

'By your leave, Colonel Lundy,' said I sharply, 'that is a subject I have no desire to hear inquired into at my table.'

'Faith, madam, I beg your pardon,' said he. 'I believe I am speaking of that which is talked of freely enough at many a table where far greater loyalty is professed; but let that pass. If it be distasteful to you, I know not why we should say another word. Only 'tis matter of common report in Dublin that the King is fled from London; if he were worth the name of King, sure, he would not desert his capital without so much as a blow struck for his rights, shamefully as he hath abused them. Such conduct cannot fail to alienate many of his most devoted subjects. It hath alienated me, and I care not who knows it.'

My lord looked both surprised and displeased. 'Sure,' said he, 'there's something in the air of your house, Hamilton, that is fatal to loyalty. First yourself, and now Lundy. It's extraordinary! How many rumours have you known, sir,' said he, turning to Lundy, 'that are utterly unfounded and false? This is another such, I dare be sworn.'

'Dare you, my lord?' says Lundy, very coolly. 'Then you dare more than I can follow you in. For where is the unlikelihood ? Does your lordship recollect what was said to you a day or two ago by one of those sturdy rebels of Enniskillen — 'twas your kinsman, Gustavus Hamilton,' said he to my husband, 'and 'twas said openly enough, since you set such store by openness. "The King," said my lord to him, when he claimed that Enniskillen was justified in taking up arms as well as Derry, because it was in self-defence—"the King will protect you." "Give me leave to tell your lordship," says he, "that the King cannot so much as protect himself." '

Lord Mountjoy might protest as he pleased ; Colonel Lundy was not to be driven from his position. The King, if he had verily fled, had cast away the allegiance of his subjects, he declared, and the subjects were consequently free to transfer their homage to another master. Not Master Jedediah Hewson himself could have maintained the position with greater openness or with greater vigour.

'Now, Mary,' said Captain Hamilton to me after they had ridden back to Derry, 'see how you have misjudged Lundy ! He may take a long time to make up his mind—and so indeed he doth, and I can't deny it—but once his mind is made up, can you say but he is as plain-spoken and as frank as any Protestant of us all ?'

CHAPTER XIX.

AFFAIRS IN DERRY.

AFTER this visit of my Lord Mountjoy's and Colonel Lundy's, we felt assured that no great severity was intended to the city for that which was past, and by consequence there seemed no reason why we should tarry longer at Cloncally. To Derry therefore we went, and found ourselves set down, as it were, in the vortex of a whirlpool. The difference was marvellous. 'Tis true that at Cloncally we seemed to ourselves to be well within the current; our thoughts were all wrapt up in the city's doings, and we had news from thence almost every day. But now we found it was but a remote cove, where scarce a breath or a swirl betokened the rush of events. We came forth from it, and were bewildered at the boiling flood.

At Cloncally every one, high and low, desired to hear all that was going on, and took a keen

interest therein ; but at Derry the very street
urchins felt themselves competent to settle the
affairs of the nation.   When friend met friend,
it was not of each other's welfare they inquired,
but whether there was more news from England
or from Dublin ; or ' Have you heard the latest
thing from Enniskillen ?' or ' Do you know what
is the last proposal my Lord Mountjoy hath
made to the Town Council ?'   There was not
a pennyworth of goods bought or sold but to
a commentary on the actions of the men that
were in power.   If any one of these walked in
the street, his name buzzed from mouth to
mouth ; and every head turned to look at him,
perhaps with respect, perhaps with derision,
according to the opinion they held of his
loyalty to the cause.   If his ears were sharp,
he might hear his actions discussed as freely
—ay, and very often with as much discern-
ment—as if his critics were his colleagues at
the council-table ; and every ragged fellow
claimed his right to think and speak on every
subject that touched the cause as freely as his
masters.

The cause was become an idol ; 'twas re-
garded by all, from the rulers to the rabble,
with a passion of devotion.   Never a man
would have grudged his life in its service, or
have held it as more than his bare duty to cast

that away, if by so doing he could further it.
'Twas a right soldier-like temper, and if, as I
have heard it said of late, it was nothing but
fear in masquerade, then never, sure, was fear
so nobly disguised. Sure, 'twas cousin-german
to that sublime fear which is the beginning of
wisdom.

It was only needful to come within the city
gates to be caught in the whirl. I had grown
proud of my citizenship before I alighted at
mine own door, I believe; by the time I had
been half an hour in the house, I was an
enthusiast like the rest. Rosa was there to
receive me, and I think we compared the
growth of our sons to the tune of 'What's
a-doing in the council?' that the boys in the
street had set us. I had come into Derry unwillingly enough, but once within the walls, I
found my place ready for me, and was glad to
be in it.

A little to my surprise, my dear father was
one of the first to welcome me back. His
temper is none of the gentlest, and I looked to
find me in disgrace, because I had rejected his
offer of a home. Nothing of the sort. It was
plain from his first word of greeting that
Captain Hamilton and I were high in his
favour, for he gave me the title of 'dear child,'
which from him is as much as multiplied

endearments from most men. To my husband
he spoke with more heartiness than I had
heard him for years.

'Is this wise of you, James?' said he—'a
man with a price upon his head to put himself
in the power of them he's opposed to without
the least necessity?'

'In their power, did you say?' said Captain
Hamilton, laughing. 'I was but now trying
to imagine what kind of bodyguard I should
raise by a cry for help. 'Twould be the wars
of Troy over again if any tried to take me out
of Derry in its present temper.'

'That is true enough,' said my father. 'One
that hath put his neck in jeopardy for the sake
of the cause is a veritable hero at the present
moment; but yet there's little use in thrusting
yourself into the very path of one that may
deem it his duty to secure you; and a riot to
rescue you might break up our negotiations in
the very moment of settlement.'

'You may keep your mind at ease on that
score, I assure you, sir,' said Captain Hamilton;
'I am but one of a crowd since the whole of
Derry joined me. What I did, they did; and
if I deserve the credit of a hero, they deserve
no less. I was broke for refusing to admit
Papists into my company; they've done exactly
the same thing, on a greater scale. If they're

to get off scot-free for it, it's like I shall fare
no worse.'

'Still the same James Hamilton, I see,' said
my father, trying to throw a tone of disapproval into his voice, but with a ray of pleasure
in the eyes that contradicted it. 'I never yet
knew you to do anything that merited praise—
or to run into anything that was worth the
name of danger.'

'And that, sure,' said Captain Hamilton,
feigning to take his meaning according to the
letter, 'is an argument of the folly of being
anxious for my safety !'

'Twas a pleasure of the purest to find my
father thus reconciled to us. All offences that
Captain Hamilton had given him in former
days, it was plain, were clean wiped out by his
action in the matter of the Papist levies. He
that had suffered for the cause, was he not a
friend to every man that had it at heart ?

Not quite, we found out later. For Mr.
Jedediah Hewson came likewise to welcome us
to the city ; only it was blame, as usual, that
he had upon his lips.

'So, madam, here you are, it seems,' said he
severely, 'after your contempt of your good
father's hospitality, which he offered you by my
mouth.'

'You should be thankful she declined the

offer, sir,' said my husband mighty gravely.
' You don't know the vixen and Termagant she
is become since her marriage, by dint of tyran-
nizing constantly over her obedient husband
and humble servant.'

' 'Tis nothing to boast of, sir,' said he, ' however true it may be.   Nor is it a proper thing
to call a woman that is a professed Christian—
of a sort—by the name of a heathen demon,
give me leave to say.'

He hath a trick most vexing to the temper,
of taking in earnest that which is said in jest.
I thought it no small proof of my meekness
that I let pass, without a word of comment,
both my husband's merry slander and his belief
in it.

' I accept your rebuke, sir,' said Captain
Hamilton, with twinkling eyes.   ' But at the
same time I must tell you that I am surprised
you are so little grateful for your escape.   You
don't know what you are spared, good Mr.
Hewson.   You'd have been at bare steel with
her by the end of the first week ; you'd have
been glad to enlist among Antrim's Red-shanks
by the second, merely for the sake of peace !'

' Sir, I perceive you are still a scoffer,' said
Mr. Hewson bitterly.   ' Doubtless you think
the position you stand in gives you a licence.
The protomartyr of this quarrel ! and one of

our deliverers! ay, sir, you may well stare, but
'tis so men hold you. Give me leave to tell
you, sir, that the Lord is not so bare of
weapons in His armoury as we of Derry, that
He should be forced to save us by means of such
as you. Had I my will, never an Episcopalian
should lift sword in our defence; no, nor any
man that has not taken the Covenant.'

And with that, he turned his back and left us
without leave-taking, which is another of his
habits when aught hath ruffled him. Dear!
how every tone and every gesture recalled the
man to my knowledge, as I had daily seen him
in my father's house before I left it.

Captain Hamilton looked at me, his eyes
brimming half with laughter and half with
astonishment.

'The man's stark mad!' said he. 'But at
least we are rid of him for once and good; and
that, as he himself would say, is matter for pro-
found thankfulness.'

'Then we must needs keep away from my
father's house,' said I. 'For there his place is
now, as it used to be, by the chimney-corner in
winter, and by the window in summer.'

Every one of the friends that came to bid us
welcome was in the same tale as my father,
about the danger Captain Hamilton ran by
putting his head into the lion's den. Captain

Browning, who came with greeting and farewell together on his lips, being in the very article of setting sail for Scotland to buy provisions; Captain Ash, his kinsman, who accompanied him; Horace Kennedy; my brother Wamphray—every one asked him the same question: 'Are you doing what is wise to be here?' On Sunday, after service, Mr. Phillips came to us in the porch of the cathedral, and spoke to him almost in the very words my father had used; which Captain Hamilton answered in much the same fashion.

'I fear, sir, that you are over-confident,' said Mr. Phillips to him. 'Were I in your shoes, I should think myself safe nowhere, save with the heads of the party, or else out of the country.'

'But, sir,' said I, speaking the wish of my heart to one that I knew had all the will to further it, 'with this talk of a general pardon to all the men of Derry, were he not best to stay where he is and cast in his lot with them? What's to hinder his name from being slipped in among the rest?'

'Why, my pretty mistress,' said our neighbour, 'I believe I speak no secret when I say it hath been tried. My lord, I know, is favourable, but for some reason he dares not be seen in it. Perhaps there's some hostile influence at work, I know not; but it's not of the least use

to name him to the Lord Deputy. Colonel
Lundy told me so himself.'

'Colonel Lundy told you so!' I repeated,
with a sinking of the heart. After the un-
reserved way in which Lundy had put himself
in our power at Cloncally, I felt it a kind of
treason to doubt him any longer; but 'twas no
easy matter to help it, when so many things
that were sorry hearing came to me in his name.

'Colonel Lundy? Yes,' said Mr. Phillips.
'He's a good enough friend to Hamilton, isn't
he?'

'Certainly, sir,' said my husband frankly.
'I've no reason to doubt it.'

I tried to repeat his words, but they stuck in
my throat in my own despite. And yet I
desired to think well of Lundy at that time, and,
what is more, I desired to avoid angering
Captain Hamilton. He came as near being
downright angry with me for this piece of
hesitation as ever he was in his life; but neither
then, when I wished to make my peace with
him, nor at this time, to Mr. Philips, could
I bring myself to say that I trusted Colonel
Lundy.

The affairs of Derry hung long in the settling;
but settled they were at last, and that to the
satisfaction of all parties. As to the articles
that were finally agreed to, there is little need

for me to recite them at length ; sure, the very
scavengers had them by heart before greater
things took their place.   Suffice it to say that
the town had all it had stood out for—both
safety and honour.   Two-thirds of my lord's
regiment, including all the new-levied men, were
to be sent back to Dublin, neither having
showed face in Derry nor struck stroke against
it.   The rest, being all Protestants and all
friends, were to all intents and purposes in-
corporated with the City Guard, so that they
became our defenders instead of our custodians.
The General Pardon was duly promised, with
confirmation under the Great Seal, as required.
If my lord had it not *in his pocket*, it seemed
that his word had power to call it forth from its
receptacle, wherever that was.   And for the
performance of that and other promises, my
lord's two sons were left hostages, while he
himself rid first to Enniskillen to pacify that
place, and then to Dublin, to ensure the re-
demption of his pledges.

What could the city desire more ? one may
well inquire.   Why, nothing ! the head-men
of the city would have been prompt to answer,
had the question been put to them at that time
—nothing, save security that the Lord Deputy
would duly perform that which had been
promised in his name by his accredited envoy.

Well, and for security, one might go on to
ask, had we not good hostages, in the persons
of my Lord Mountjoy's two sons that I spoke
of but a minute ago ?   No doubt, had the Lord
Deputy been anybody else under the sun, that
had seemed sufficient warrandice to reasonable
men of all sides.   But 'lying Dick Talbot,' was
he not known among us ?   Why, the mere fact
that a promise had been made in his name to
them he counted rebels, was it not like to be a
temptation to him to go counter to it ?   And as
to hostages, was he one to be tender of their
lives ?   Were they the sons of his dearest
friend (and we shortly had reason to know that
he held the Lord Mountjoy far otherwise), would
he hesitate to sacrifice them if care of them
should be any curb upon his plans ?

Thus, my lord Viscount had no sooner
turned his back upon us, than news began
to come in from all sides that was enough to
disquiet the babes in their cradles and the dead
in their graves.   Potents issued to all the
notable Papists in the kingdom to levy Irish
troops to the very utmost of their ability, the
captains to pay nothing for their commissions,
but, instead, to support their men for three
months at their own expense.   Many a man
was dull enough to laugh at that provision when
he heard it, knowing that it was more than the

most of these fine captains could do to support themselves. In a very few days they were laughing, as the vulgar saying hath it, *on the other side of their mouths.* For, as they might have known at the first hearing of it, they that had no means of their own to subsist their companies were nothing loath to subsist them on the means of their neighbours. The troops were Rapparees and robbers of old, near every man of them ; now they robbed with authority, having Tyrconnel's commission for it.

Nor could they now pretend the King's service as a justification, for it was everywhere known that he was fled into France. That which Colonel Lundy had told us at Cloncally as a rumour was subject of common talk through the province, and his commentary on it was likewise in the mouths of the very rabble—' If that be the quality of the King, is he one that deserves our obedience ?'

The flight of the country-folk into Derry had all but ceased, when the 9th of December came and passed so harmlessly. Now it began again, like the flowing of a tide, every wave a terrified Protestant family ; nor terrified only by rumour, but able to cite both date and doer of outrages enough to have raised, not terror merely, but panic. And all this, when my Lord

Mountjoy had newly left us, after assuring us of security against that very thing.

But if the Lord Deputy took us for infants, to be satisfied with fair words and quieted with promises, while our ruin was evidently aimed at and openly encouraged, he was now to find out his mistake. The men of Derry were not of that tame nature at any time, that can be treated so with safety. And at this time their natural high spirit was chafed into a very fervour of mingled enthusiasm and indignation. Sure, my Lord Mountjoy knew that very well. Had Tyrconnel but waited for his report, he had never acted so like the fool in the story, that puts the lighted brand into the midst of the dry tinder.

The province of Ulster was that tinder, and burst incontinent into flame. Tyrconnel's levies were met by levies on the other side. His licensed marauders presently found the country purged of the helpless and the timid, and where they came looking for nothing but a passive prey, they found instead armed and resolute men, fully minded to defend themselves and their goods.

Captain Hamilton was not the man to sit idle at home while there was fighting around him ; he had certainly been up and away to join his friends at the first rumour of it, even without

being summoned.   But summoned he was, and
that by his good friend Sir Arthur Rawdon,
a letter from whom was put into his hands on
the 26th of December.   It ran thus :

'Moyra, *December the 24th.*

'MY DEAR SIR,

'You being the man you are, I believe I
shall tell you no news, or only such as you are
daily looking for, when I do you to wit of a
meeting that is to be held on the 27th day of
this instant month, here at my house of Moyra.
Some of the chief men of the Protestant party
are to be present, and matters will be handled
that are of great concernment to all of us.
Should this come to your hands in time, your
presence and counsel will be highly esteemed
by, my dear sir,

'Yours, etc., etc., etc.,

'A. RAWDON.'

Upon receipt of that letter, be sure there was
a sudden calling to horse and a hurried leave-
taking.   And I, for my part, was glad to see
him depart, having by that time heard so much
of the danger he ran by being in Derry, that I
had begun almost to believe in it.   The one
thing I feared for him, and that I begged him
to beware of, was that he should be led into
some fresh piece of imprudence.   For Sir

Arthur Rawdon, as all the world knows, is a man brave far beyond the edge of rashness. What to hesitating tempers seems on the extreme verge of possibility, appears to him the most feasible thing in the world—nay, easy and ordinary. And Captain Hamilton resembles him but too closely in that. I besought him, of his love for me, to have a care.

'Why, Mary,' said he, 'what a little coward you are grown! Will it be possible, I wonder, to make Scotch blood comprehend that there's a time when caution is the worst of all rashness?'

'Ah!' said I, 'but that's not the sort of caution that I advocate. And can I, I wonder, convince blood, as Scotch as my own at least, that there's a kind of rashness which is *rash?*'

He laughed.

'Why, no doubt,' said he; 'but that, you see, is not the kind of rashness that I shall countenance.'

This was a fair answer, and I laughed in my turn.

'Don't you see,' he continued, 'don't you know, that we have done enough already to put our necks in the noose? There's not a Rap in the country but can tell you that the penalty's no greater for stealing a sheep than for stealing a lamb.'

'Oh,' said I, 'here's a fine ill-omened image, to be sure! Here's pretty comfort indeed for a poor woman that sees her husband about to ride away to help to organize sedition!'

'And that's a pretty word,' said he, 'from the mouth of the wife of Captain James Hamilton of Cloncally, the proscribed Protestant; and the daughter of one of the most prominent Non conformists in Derry; not to say a young lady that hath fought with her own hands in the same cause!'

'Not quite,' said I, 'though I own I did something very near it.'

'Well,' said he, 'perhaps you will do it entirely before these troubles are entirely past. I little doubt but you'll have occasion, if you desire it; for all Mountjoy and his Articles. I'd give something considerable, I may tell you in confidence, to see these same Articles in Lundy's hands, duly ratified under Tyrconnel's hand and seal.'

As to Lundy's part in these stirrings, it was up to this time a passive one. He encouraged all that was done by the Protestant gentry to secure themselves; but he lifted no finger to help them. And that was a thing he might have done with very good effect, being our Governor, as Lord Mountjoy's substitute, in the room of George Phillips of Newtown. There were some few of us that had been better pleased had the last-named gentleman been continued in that post, and Lundy held only his natural command of the troops. But, in truth, we were so few, and the appointment was so very natural, that we were even fain to hold our peace, and to strive to believe Lundy as good a friend to the cause as he professed himself.

We strove; and we forbore so much as to hint at any misgiving; and as to Colonel Lundy, his professions were as great as professions could well be. But there were two or three of us that found our doubts of him tough to kill. To such as had looked him fairly in the eyes, at a moment when the natural man was uppermost, confidence in Lundy was a plant of slow and delicate growth, and one that needed both care and artifice in the rearing. Mistrust of him, on the other hand, was one native to the soil, which it filled with its spreading roots. Let but the least cause in life be given, and the exotic were suddenly overrun past finding, and choked past recovery.

But yet how plain he spoke! how openly he took part with us, and that in any company! Why, I myself heard him say a thing that made me ashamed of mine own suspicious doubts. It was in my father's house on the evening of the 1st of January. Wamphray had ridden back

from the conference at Moyra to summon as many
men as we could get together to follow himself
and Captain Hamilton to the field.   Even by
this time, so soon after our arrival in Derry,
'twas become a kind of custom of mine to spend
an hour in my father's house every evening;
sure, I was little like to pretermit it when there
was news to be had of my husband.   Presently
Mr. Lundy came in, desiring Wamphray's news
of the business the confederacy had in hand,
and comparing it with what he had learnt from
others that were come back to Derry upon the
same errand.   And being asked for my opinion
on some point or other, I could not forbear to
deplore the pass things were come to before we
knew what was Tyrconnel's answer to my Lord
Mountjoy.   Rosa followed me in it.

'Why, 'tis none of our fault,' said Colonel
Lundy, with some heat.   'We are put in that
position that we have no choice but to take
arms in our own defence.   And give me leave
to tell you, ladies both, that it's no bad way to
secure good terms from Tyrconnel to treat with
him armed.   He is one that may be brought to
accept that which he would hardly grant.'

'Like enough,' said my father approvingly.
'Let him be glad to do, for his own sake, what
we desire, and then there is a chance that he
will not go back from his word.'

'You put it exactly,' responded Colonel Lundy.

Wamphray looked at him keenly.

'Have you heard who are appointed our commanders?' he asked.

'My Lord Mount-Alexander to command the forces from Down and Antrim,' said Lundy, checking them off upon his fingers, 'and Skeffington second to him; my Lord Kingston those of Sligo, and Chidley Coote second to him; my Lord Blaney those of Armagh and Monaghan. I haven't heard the name of his lieutenant. Is there any other chosen to command?'

'You are yourself mentioned,' said Wamphray, 'as the likeliest person to hold command of the forces in Derry, Tyrone, and Donegal; with a kind of general authority over the whole confederacy. Have you heard nothing of it?'

'Not a word,' said Colonel Lundy composedly. ''Tis even far too high an honour for me; but in that position, should it be accorded to me, or in any other, the Confederacy may count upon my whole strength, my best efforts, in their interest.'

After that, were it not a kind of slur upon one's own honesty to doubt the man? And yet I caught myself wondering if he was

entirely and heartily our friend.   And that
there were one or two more of my mind I knew
well enough, though to name a suspicion in my
father's house had been as much as my welcome
there was worth.

About the middle of the month there came
at last to the town my Lord Mountjoy's long-
expected letter, assuring us, in the first place,
of the Lord Deputy's acceptance of his articles
with us, and telling us, in the second, of his
mission into France to obtain the King's leave
to treat with the Prince of Orange for the
kingdom.   As the substance of that letter
leaked out, the ferment in Derry, that had
been a little allayed by diverse contending
interests, boiled up again as fierce as at first.
And thus it happened that, meeting my cousin,
Adam Murray, in the street, we fell to talking
of that letter before ever we asked each other
of the health of our relations.   Before Adam
had said ten words, I knew that he trusted
Lundy as little as I.

'That letter,' said he, 'hath treachery upon
the face of it.'

'Not on the part of my Lord Mountjoy, I'm
certain,' said I.

'On Mountjoy's part?   No,' said Adam.
'But he's hoodwinked, or I'm much mistaken.
Why, what end is served, supposing Tyrconnel

to be honest with us, by his promising through
Mountjoy to ratify the Articles? None. The
ratification itself might be in our hands as easy
as the promise. Mountjoy hath granted us
terms too favourable, and I fear he is being
sent out of the way to leave Tyrconnel a free
hand to crush us at his leisure.'

' I like not Rice for my lord's colleague,'
said I.

' I think nothing of that,' said Adam.
' Mountjoy's letter said it was the very contrary that was thought in Dublin—that he
himself was no fit colleague for Rice, and that
'twas less than courteous to send even one
commissioner to the King that was not of his
own faith.'

' I wish they had stuck to that,' said I.

Adam smiled.

' I wish no less,' said he. ' But, still, it's not
that which disquiets me. Rice's wishes and
leanings may be what they please, but Mountjoy
hath weight enough to keep him straight if
things be as they are represented.'

' Ah,' said I, ' there's the point; if things be
as they are represented. Where's cause to
show for doubting it? None that one can see
or can state. And yet—and yet—how can one
help but doubt!'

' No cause!' said Adam. ' There's cause in

plenty, and fit enough to be stated, too, if there were any use in stating it.   Why, the half of Mountjoy's letter was filled with that very thing; combating doubts that he saw were sure to arise.   He seems perfectly sure that no trickery is intended; I would I shared his confidence, that's all.'

'But, after all,' said I, 'we have the security of Mountjoy's faith, which is another thing than Tyrconnel's promise.   He will return from France, and then he'll be to reckon with, if his agreement with us have not been carried out.'

'When! *If!*' said Adam, shaking his head. 'It's a long way to France, Mary.   There are possibilities that one does not like to contemplate.'

This was a new thought to me, and one that touched the springs of my memory.   As in a picture, I saw once more the eyes of Lundy, when he had received an answer from Mountjoy at mine own table, that might be made a handle of.

'And if there's any treachery intended to my lord himself,' said I, 'then, mark my words, Adam, it's not Tyrconnel that is the arch-traitor, but another that hath his ear.'

He looked at me strangely.

'That hath crossed my own mind, and more than once while we've been speaking,' said he.

'Oh, and I wish he may be as good a friend to
the cause as he professes.' He paused for a
moment, and then went on, as one that talks to
himself: 'He hath given little cause for distrust that one can lay hold of. And yet I am
persuaded that 'tis his own interest he desires
to serve, not ours. The man's a fox, not a
doubt of that. But we are no geese, to be his
victims; hounds, rather, to keep him within
bounds, and to protect the homesteads that are
our charge.'

Alas and alas! 'tis an ill omen for the homesteads when the fox is mounted on the hunts-
man's saddle, and hath whip and bugle given
him to guide the hounds withal.

CHAPTER XX.

THE ANTRIM ASSOCIATION.

BUT to breathe a word of such a suspicion in
my father's house had been, as I said, to
imperil my welcome there   That, I promise
you, was a thing I had no mind to risk, for
there was no house in Derry where more was
to be learnt of that which was a-doing either
in the city or in the field.   Mr. Murray, though
a Nonconformist, and consequently a man who
held no office in the town, was much looked
up to by all sorts, and had friends among all
parties.   Was there a reinforcement leaving
the city? 'twas odds but the officer was a
friend of his, and drew rein at the door to bid
him farewell.   Was there a council holding?
some man that had a seat at the board was
sure to desire Mr. Murray's good counsel.
Were there despatches sent in to Derry from
the front? there was sure to be some com-
munication directed to his hands; and he that

brought it—if, as was most likely, he came straight from the Governor's house—was ready to tell over not only the tidings from the army, but all that had passed in Lundy's house as well.

Thus I came more and more to frequent my father's house, mine being floated by the fortune of war into the back-swirl of the eddy, and the news that came to it like to be both tardy and garbled. And news of the army was become a very staple of life to us stay-at-homes—as necessary as bread to eat or air to breathe.

Here it was that Mr. Skeffington found me, when at the very beginning of the campaign he rid into Derry with news of the attempt upon Lisburn, that was the first of our actions against the Catholics. He had very kindly taken charge of a letter from Captain Hamilton to me, and it was little I heard of his talk with my father and Rosa until I finished reading that letter. I knelt down beside the fire, and, heedless of Mr. Hewson's eyes regarding me from his place—his own acknowledged place— in the opposite corner thereof, I read it through by the light of the flickering blaze.

This was the letter:

'Belfast, *January the 9th*, 1688.

'SWEETHEART,

'Skeffington, that rides this day to Derry (I would it were I in his place), hath promised to do you to wit of our attempt upon Lisburn and Carrickfergus, wherein, upon the whole, we have failed; it was well planned and well begun, but was spoilt by the backwardness of the men of Belfast, that are too apt to be trimming when they should be doing. They watch the balance; sure, they have swords in their hands, and these, well wielded, will weigh up all the lead in the world. Our army grows apace, notwithstanding; I know one lady that will follow it every day with her prayers, specially now that there appears good likelihood of succours from England, which may enable us to hold our own with the Irish; perhaps to turn the tables on them — who knows?

'Leighton is sent into England with letters to the Prince, and I am ordered to go with him to buy us arms and powder. 'Tis much against my will that I depart from the air you breathe in, though there be miles betwixt us here; nor is time allowed me to ride to Derry to take farewell of you. No matter; 'twill be but the happier meeting when I return.

'And I would not be like these same trimmers of Belfast, who would sooner risk their treasure than themselves in defence of it. Mine, as well you know, is ever on the spot of ground that you inhabit, and 'tis hard to go

without seeing that the same is safe; but a
soldier that hath his orders must not linger,
and it is matter of some pride to me to be
chosen for so great a trust.

'I commend you, sweetest and dearest, to
the keeping of our Almighty Defence, and so
farewell. That He may have you in the safety
of His keeping is the prayer, mine own sweet
wife [which is as much as a man can say, and
worth all other terms of endearment put
together],

'Of your loving husband and servant,

'JAMES HAMILTON.

'Kiss Roland for me. The things you sent
me by Cargill came safe to hand, and were
most welcome and most useful.'

The reading of that letter carried me out
from the dimly-lighted room, beyond the city
wall, to the camp, and the open sea, and the
English coast. Back to the four walls that
enclosed us I came with a bound as I finished
it, and the first words that fell upon mine ears
were Rosa's.

'Then bad's the best of your news, Mr.
Skeffington,' said she.

'Sure, not altogether,' said I to myself, for
if he were sent far away from me, at least he
was put in the position of trust that was his due.

'I marvel that you will say so, Mrs. Murray,' said Mr. Skeffington in reply to her, and a little beside my thought. 'They're mixed, at the worst, and hope is the chief ingredient of the mixture. We won at Lisburn, if the rest of the project failed, and even so a third of their men, or near it, have come over to us since the attempt. We shall be victors in the end ; never doubt it.'

So 'twas the general business they were upon, not that particular one that had filled all my sky for the moment. 'What a fool I am !' I said to myself. And the eyes of Mr. Hewson, meeting mine at that moment, affirmed my verdict, with enlargements.

'Besides,' Mr. Skeffington continued, 'we are hardly come to actual warfare yet. Friday's affair was more in the nature of persuasion than of compulsion—a declaration of our determination to defend ourselves rather than the opening of a vigorous campaign. And—a word in your ear—'tis more than likely that the demonstration may prove all that's necessary. Tyrconnel is none so ready to meet us, even with all the advantage he hath. And why, I pray you? Why, but because even he begins to see that the best thing he can do is to make terms with the Prince of Orange peaceably.'

'Under your favour, Mr. Skeffington, I

doubt that hugely,' said Mr. Murray. 'The
Lord Deputy is one whose intentions cannot
be gauged by his professions, remember that;
no, nor by the minds of honest men at all, I
believe. I would not advise that guile should
be met with guile, but assuredly it should be
met with the most guarded carefulness.'

'Set a thief to catch a thief, you would say?'
said Mr. Skeffington meditatively.

He received Mr. Murray's words with so
much attention that it showed me afresh how
his counsel was esteemed.

'" Be ye wiser than serpents" would be a
fitter expression, sir, from the mouth of a
captain in the army of the Lord,' said Mr.
Hewson, with severity.

'You don't go on to recommend the harmlessness of the dove, sir, I perceive,' said Mr.
Skeffington, laughing.

''Tis the wrong time for it,' said Mr. Murray
gravely. 'Take my word for it, sir, there is
no surer way to provoke violence than to show
yourselves unprepared to repel it, nor no better
way to preserve that same harmlessness than
to show the serpent his fangs are outmatched
should you be put to using yours.'

'Then, 'tis set a thief to catch a thief, after
all, with the deepest respect to Mr. Hewson,'
said Mr. Skeffington, rising to go. 'But where

are we to find a serpent for the office? We
be all good men and true on our side, I am
well assured.'

So they thought at that time, both soldiers
and citizens. There be men in plenty that will
tell you now they suspected Lundy from the
first; if that be true, I have no more to say
than that they showed a singular great talent
for concealing their suspicions. When he was
named Commander-in-Chief of the Protestant
forces in the North—the Lords Mount-Alexander, Blaney, and Kingston, and Sir Arthur
Rawdon, all agreeing to submit to him as the
central authority — was there a voice lifted
against it? Not one; the appointment was
well received everywhere and by all sorts.

Nay, was not I myself all but publicly
reproved by George Phillips the Sunday next
after Mr. Skeffington brought the news into
town of that very attempt upon Carrickfergus
that I have just recounted? We were gathered
in little groups in the churchyard after service
to discuss it; 'twas a habit we were fallen into
about that time of gathering in little knots at
that place and time to talk over the affairs of
the nation. The tidings of our failure in that
first attempt was ill received upon the whole,
and there arose such a chorus of expressions of
confidence in Lundy — 'Lundy would have

done this,' 'Lundy will now do that,' and
' Had Lundy been in the field there had been
another tale to tell'—that to one who remembered that Lundy had as yet done nothing at
all, save to sit at home in quiet, it became
ridiculous.

' Why, so he will, no doubt,' I let slip in
mere carelessness, 'if he be as good a friend to
us as he professes.'

Every face turned to me with a different
depth of wonder printed on it.

' Have you any cause to doubt him?' Mr.
Phillips asked me.

' Why, no,' I found myself obliged to answer;
'none that I can mention, or that is worth the
stating.'

He bowed with a grave countenance. But
as we were dispersing he came to my side, and
' Madam,' says he, in a tone of voice that was
meant for mine own ear only, 'so old a friend
as I am may perhaps be pardoned if he offers
a suggestion that you may think a bold one.'

' I beg you'll make it,' I replied, knowing
well what he was about to say.

' Well, then,' said he, 'a suspicion that rests
upon so slight a cause that it can't be stated is
a suspicion that it's hardly wise to glance at,
even in private talk.'

I had done it in public, and could have bitten

the foolish tongue that had earned me blame
from a man whose esteem I valued.

This was the temper of the town with respect
to Lundy in the middle of January, but a month
later it was greatly changed. By that time
there were many whose faces grew as long at
the mention of his name as mine had done in
January; and there were some that stuck not to
mutter a prayer for his honesty, that was much
like a curse in disguise. Little marvel! There
is no man, I suppose, that can always be acting,
and Lundy had once or twice permitted his
mask of dove to slip aside and the serpent
below to peep out. As, for instance, when he
issued his proclamation discharging the city
bands from keeping guard with his own
soldiers, and their own officers from bearing
command over them, a thing which cost him
the allegiance of many that before it would
have answered for his honesty with their lives.

But even after that the balance of opinion
among the leaders continued in his favour; pity
alike and marvel that it was so. When I look
back upon the whole events of that gloomy
winter—the soddenest I can remember, and as
gloomy and depressing in its events as in its
weather—it is hard to believe that the gentry
of Ulster endured his authority till the end of
it. Yet they did so, well-nigh to their ruin.

Do but think of it. 'Twas one disaster on the back of another, one discouragement following on the heels of the last. From that attempt upon Lisburn—that I have just related—to the last engagement at Claudy Ford before the investment, was there one affair that was well managed? Was there one wherein we were fairly matched and fairly worsted? Not one.

Everywhere in the province single parties of our men beat equal or greater numbers of the Raps and Ultoghs they were opposed to; could have beaten them, as Sir Arthur ('the Cock of the North,' as they called him) put it to me, with one hand. But yet throughout the province we made no ground, even before Richard Hamilton came against us. After his coming, it was dead leaves before the wind we were like. Driven from one post to another back upon our places of strength, and then back again from these upon the central fortress of Derry, often without a blow struck or a shot fired, so that it began to appear as though the very name of an army was more than we had heart to withstand. And for all this who was mainly to blame?

Ask any man in the kingdom to-day, and he will be at no loss for his answer. If he be one that loves fair dealing, he will not seek to disguise the fact that the Consult at Hillsborough

were over-confident, both in their own power
and in Tyrconnel's fear of them, so that they
neglected many precautions they should have
taken good heed to.   But neither can he hide
the other certainty, that for one mischance that
over-confidence led to, twenty were caused by
sheer base treachery—he that had undertaken
to lead them, leading them, not merely astray,
but of set purpose into the toils of the enemy.

Ask Sir Arthur Rawdon else; he who made
efforts almost more than human to get men
together in competent numbers in the places
where they were like to be needed, and at the
end was left with four or five hundred men at
Loughbricklan to face the whole bulk of Richard
Hamilton's army.   And when, falling back from
thence upon Dromore, he was served at last
with the powder and shot that had been withheld from him till he was in the very presence
of the enemy, what did he find ?   That the
bullets were unsuitable to the unsizeable arms
of his men, so that they were all the same as
unarmed, as well as outmatched by nearly ten
to one.   Is it any marvel they broke and fled ?
And yet Lundy scrupled not to use in Sir
Arthur's hearing—as he told me with angry
tears in his eyes—the insulting title of 'the
break of Dromore,' which the enemy bestowed
on his defeat.

Ask my Lord Mount - Alexander, he who would have joined Sir Arthur at Loughbricklan except for Lundy's charge that he should wait his arrival at Hillsborough, where he promised to join him with at the least a thousand men properly appointed, and a train of artillery besides. Such a reinforcement would have made victory a certainty, so that, even apart from the obedience due to the orders of the Commander-in-Chief, 'twas clearly my lord's duty to wait for them. If he waited too long, so that his forces joined Sir Arthur's only in time to retreat along with them; and if the provision he had laid up at Hillsborough for his own and Lundy's men fell into the hands of the Irish army in the very nick of their need, whose is the fault?

Ask my Lord Kingston, who was ordered by Lundy to quit Sligo and hasten to Derry, upon a lying pretext of immediate need, at the very moment when his plans were beginning to bear fruit, and his troops to be felt as a complete check upon the enemy's advance. No sooner was he out of it than they took possession; the forts that had been built and repaired to resist them became a protection to them; and the key of Connaught was in their hands. And Lord Kingston was not even permitted to enter Derry with his troops, to give a colour of reality to the pretence upon which he had been ordered out of Sligo, but left at Ballyshannon without being afforded another chance of striking a blow for the cause he had at heart.

Ask Ensign McClelland and Cornet Nicholson, who rode into Derry together to buy powder for the troops in the field, and paid for it, too, at the rate of five pounds the barrel; but never saw a grain of it from then till now, in spite of Lundy's promise to send it after them forthwith.

But why should I multiply instances? 'Tis one tale everywhere. Two things were paramount necessities to our raw and poorly-appointed men—to wit, heartening and furnishing. Did they get either from Lundy? No; but promises of supplies and of reinforcements left purposely unfulfilled, that hope deferred might sicken the highest heart; and as to encouragement, was it not constantly told them that they were unfit to face a regular army; till, disparagement joining with actual failure to dispirit them, they began to believe it?

'Tis nothing to the purpose to urge, as I have heard it urged, that Lundy still bore King James's commission, and consequently was bound to serve him. If he was so, he was bound also to let it be known. Cormack O'Neill bore King James's commission, too;

but he left his mayoralty of Derry and became a colonel in the Irish army. There was no uncertain ring about Nugent, neither; nor yet about Patrick Sarsfield; nor fifty others that I could name. The truth is, that a gentleman might be a Protestant and yet a Tory, but none could be a gentleman and yet a traitor. And what was it to entice the whole Protestant interest of the North into one ship (as one might figure it) and that ship entrusted to his pilotage; and then to steer it straight and deliberately upon the rocks? There never was treason but one that was blacker since the beginning of the world.

I might multiply instances by the dozen, and yet never go beyond those I heard narrated by persons concerned. But the case of Dungannon is typical, and so I give it; the more as it was the cause of Mr. Walker's coming to Derry, a thing which turned so greatly to our help in after-days.

Dungannon is a place that was shrewdly threatened by the Irish garrison in Charlemont, so that it was thought necessary to secure it by a good garrison of its own. Accordingly it was fortified by a good number of troops under Colonel Stewart and the Rev. George Walker, Rector of Donaghmore. Early in February Mr. Walker rid to Derry to consult with

Colonel Lundy about its defence, who approved
and encouraged the design, and sent them two
companies of his disciplined men, together with
orders to collect as great a store of provision as
they could; which was done. A great stock of
victual was got together, fair payment being
made for all that was brought in; and the raids
of the marauders at Charlemont so well checked,
that they, having no money to buy stores, and
finding it impossible to take them by force as
formerly, were fain to shift their quarters or
to starve. In the middle of March, when
Richard Hamilton's troops were driving all
before them, and when a defeat of the Irish
by our men had been especially valuable as
putting heart into the rest, what must our
Commander-in-Chief do? What, but to send
orders to the garrison at Dungannon to quit
that place, and that in such haste that all their
stores must be left behind. Faith and indeed!
it was no less than a godsend to the starving
Papists at Charlemont, that walked in without
striking a blow, and enjoyed that which to save
their lives they could not have taken. Mr.
Walker with his troop rid in to Derry, and to
hear him, as with burning indignation and resentment he related the whole, one could no
have believed that he would ever again be
upon terms with his betrayer. But behold a

marvel! A little dexterous explanation given, and a little flattery applied by Lundy, and there were the two as friendly, to all seeming, as before, riding out together to Coleraine to view the shattered remains of the Protestant army.

CHAPTER XXI.

TELLS HOW MRS. HAMILTON AND OTHERS RECEIVED
HAPPY NEWS AND HARSH REBUKES.

HOWEVER sodden the weather, it cannot be
always raining; there will be gleams of sun-
shine in the gloomiest day; and sometimes
in the depth of winter there comes one that
is bright with the promise of spring. And
however ruthless the evil fortune, there will
sometimes be happy chances. As winter cannot last for ever, so 'tis a long lane (as the
proverb tells us) that hath no turning. But as
there be many days compounded both of winter
and spring, rain and shine by turns, so perhaps
there may be chances wherein good and evil
are so mixed and mingled that 'tis hard to say
which hath the upper hand.

When our men began to return, by twos and
threes, from their disheartening campaign, it
was this last kind of chance. In that they had
fared no better, was matter enough for grief;

but in that they came back safe and sound, was
equal matter for joy. The mind we were put
into was the very match of the young spring's,
that laughed and cried at once. But hope was
stirring with the stirring of the sap, and, touch-
ing the balance, inclined it to the sunward side.

'Twas true that we had lost—lost battles
more than one, and lost ground throughout the
province. But there was one thing we had not
lost—and that was heart ; we were not beaten
yet, nor near it. Very few of our men were
killed ; some were hurt, but even of wounded
there were not many. Our army would quickly
draw together again, and meet Richard Hamilton on more equal terms ; forewarned, they tell
us, is forearmed ; we knew our own weaknesses,
and how to take order against them, perhaps
also we knew theirs, which was more to the
purpose. Soon would come the turning of the
lane ; soon there would be another tale to tell.
And after that would follow home-comings that
should have no blemish of failure on their joy.

So we told Wamphray, when he rid home
much depressed, after Dromore ; and he believed it, nothing loath, and was all on fire to
have at the enemy once more.

'We were sold into their hands at Dromore,'
said he—'sold, and perhaps bought ; I could
well believe it. Deceived by Tyrconnel's pre-

tence of a desire to avoid actual fighting until
the King's pleasure should be known; that at
the first; and afterwards betrayed—there's no
other word for it—into Hamilton's hands.   But
you're right in saying that there will be another
tale to tell next time we meet him; there will,
or my name's not Wamphray Murray.'

Soon after Wamphray's return, and before he
had rid back to join Sir Arthur Rawdon on the
Bann. there was a blither home-coming; Mr.
Browning's, to wit, who came back from Scotland with a very welcome cargo of victual.   It
fell out, by chance, that Mrs. Browning was in
my house when Margery brought in the rumour
that the *Mountjoy* was in Ross's Bay.   Straight
she fell to wondering 'was it true,' her grand-
child, little Mary Rankin, running up to our
knees with Roland, to ask the same question of
us, who knew no more than they did.

'Why,' said I to Mrs. Browning, 'there's one
certain means to test its truth.'

'Sure enough,' she rejoined, laughing; 'and
that's as much as to say, I may go and see!   I
would, too, had I anyone to bear me company.'

'I'll do that same with pleasure,' said I.
'The children will be perfectly safe and happy
with Margery; come, let us go at once.'

No sooner said than done.   In a moment we
were cloaked and hooded, and the next we were

making the best of our way across the Diamond
and down Silver Street to the Ship Quay Gate,
where we found ourselves in the midst of a
small crowd of persons, desiring leave to pass
out upon the same errand as our own. They
were mostly persons of the baser sort, who no
doubt had friends among the crew ; and it did
flash briskly through my mind that things were
come to a pretty pass, when Mrs. Hamilton ot
Cloncally, and Mrs. Browning, her friend, were
mixing in such a crowd, at such a place and
such an hour—for 'twas after sunset—and that
without so much as a servant at their heels to
show their quality. Faith, Mrs. Hamilton and
Mrs. Browning were soon to learn, along with
others their equals and their betters, their perfect kindred with the meanest blood in Derry ;
and that by sharper means than a little jostling.

As to the rumour, 'twas as true as that it was
spoken ; for even as we came upon the quay,
the *Mountjoy* was in the article of coming
alongside. Her captain stood upon the poop,
giving his words of command, pointing the
same and directing his men with his sword,
which he held bare in his hand. The next
moment came the rattle and plunge of the
anchor, as it was let go ; and a little buzz of
satisfaction ran through the crowd, a pleasant
sound and a friendly. Then began a calling of

greetings from the quay to the vessel and back
again, that likewise was pleasant hearing. So
far as I saw, there was not another person of
condition on the quay but ourselves ; but for all
that, the crowd was composed of honest and
friendly people ; and I did not hesitate to ask
Mrs. Browning if she had any objection to be
left among them, while I went to carry the good
news to Rosa; to which she answered, 'No.'   I
had, indeed, no wish to intrude upon her meeting with her husband, that five minutes more
must bring to pass.

The first person I saw in my father's house
was Wamphray.   When Rosa came flying
down the stairs to hear my news, he put his
arm round her, and so they stood listening.
A kind of sorry jealousy traversed my heart as
I saw it.   Here was Wamphray come home to
his wife with honour, though unsuccessful ;
there on the quay was her brother, come home
with both honour and success, having brought
in the victual he was sent for.   When was my
turn coming, I wondered?   When would
Captain Hamilton come in to the quay, having
done, I whispered to myself, not merely the
thing he went to do, but something more ? for
it was ever his way to go beyond the thing
that was asked of him, if going beyond were
possible.

'Well,' I said to them, having told mine errand, 'I'd best be getting home now, as it seems to me.'

'You deserve to be taken at your word, for that saying,' said Rosa, smiling round about at each of us. 'Well you know your absence would make a gap it would take much of our pleasure to fill up; but I have more than half a mind to tell you to get you home for a kill-joy, all the same, to punish you for talking nonsense.'

Her face was all aglow, her eyes alight with the pleasure of my good news; but in upon her happy voice—as if joy were a spell to conjure him up, to its own destruction—broke Mr. Hewson's stern one :

' 'Tis an excellent good saying, Mrs. Murray, though I doubt you meant it but in jest, that such false speeches deserve their punishment. Ay, and they shall have it, too!'—and with that word he turned a frowning countenance upon me—'they shall have it, or I am no true prophet.'

For my life, I could not help but quail before his face of stern authority, though I made a shift to answer him lightly.

'Methinks, sir," I told him, 'you are over-hard upon a silly little saying, scarce meant in earnest.'

' "Jesting and foolish talking, which are not

convenient,"' he quoted mighty harshly. ' 'Tis
no more than may be looked for from you, and
such as you, for all that. 'Twas idle in me to
chide you, for well I know that you will never
amend at my reproof; but give me leave to tell
you to your fair false face that falseness is
never a trifle, madam, were you twice as fair as
you be.'

Therewith, and with a bow that condensed
whole volumes of reprobation, he quitted the
room. I tried to laugh, though with little mirth,
for, truth to tell, his manner had daunted me
for once. But Rosa was in a blaze of indignation.

'You're right, Mary,' said she. 'Our submission hath clean turned the man's head.
What hath he to do to break out on one of us
in such a manner, even if we were false in
earnest? None. 'Tis we that have spoilt him,
till he hath lost all idea of his place.'

I thought it even but too likely; and so we
rang the changes on his tyranny for a time,
until, as such bubblings of discontent had always
ended, so this ended in its turn.

'He is a good man, though harsh,' said
Wamphray, 'and we must even forgive the
harshness for the sake of the goodness.'

'Twas the old story, and it had been but idle
breath for me to have said aught to the con-

trary. But I fell a-musing, why that temper of restraint and gloom should be thought more proper to human goodness than one of sweet human mirth, and for all my musing I could find no answer. No ; nor have ever found one since, though 'tis often and often I have pondered the same question.

I stayed with them against my will. I was over-paid for my compliance by the sight of the very gladdest meeting that ever I was witness to. And yet scarce a word beyond the very commonplace of greeting ; the sympathy between these twin souls was so perfect as to make words wholly superfluous. Scarce a caress ; and yet what a light in their eyes, on their faces! the dusky room seemed brightened by it ; we that stood by rejoiced in it. Never, sure, were brother and sister that loved each other more absolutely. A great thankfulness sprang up in my soul to God, that whatever pain He hath ordained in this world for discipline, He hath ordained love also, which is discipline and reward in one.

Mine own turn came next, and speedily.

' Here's Mrs. Hamilton, that ran away from me on the quay. I did not think I was such a bugbear!' said he ; but there was a kindly gleam in his eyes that belied his words.

' I ran away,' I said, ' merely to bring Rosa

the news of your return. Why should she be deprived of the pleasure of knowing it, even for a quarter of an hour?'

'It was kindly done of you,' said he, releasing my hand. 'And yet I warrant you had lingered, had you had the least inkling of one piece of news I bring.'

At that, I promise you, the blood came burning into my cheeks.

'Out with it! hasten!' said Rosa, clasping her hands over her brother's shoulder. 'Let us hear it at once, lest it lose its savour through delay.'

'That it can't do,' said I. And even to myself my voice sounded strangely soft as I said it—a kind of liquid joy, a kind of spoken smiling. 'For there's but one article of news that would be worth the telling in the midst of such happiness, and that's the news of my husband's return. I—I see it in your eyes!' I finished, looking at him.

'So you may,' said he, 'for it's true;' and his kind face beamed as he said it. 'I hailed a ship that we passed in the Lough; you know our mariner fashion. She comes on slowly, and no marvel; for she's deeply laden. She hails the *Jersey* frigate, of London; Captain Beverly. She's laden with powder and arms for Derry, in charge of—whom do you think?'

'Why, of Captain Hamilton of Cloncally, that went for it,' said Rosa. 'Whom else?'

'Of Captain James Hamilton, as sure as you've said it,' said Captain Browning, radiant.

'Ah!' said Rosa, drawing a long breath; 'it seemed a minute ago as though my cup of happiness were full to the brim; but I find there was room in it for another drop, and that's this.' With that she cast her arms round me with a kiss; it was mine own thought of five minutes before given back to me. The gladness I had felt at her gladness, sure, she felt the same for mine. Was it not a joy as precious and as wholesome to our souls as any rod?

Straight, as that thought formed itself in my mind, broke in upon it my father's stern voice, raised in reproof of us; though sure am I there had never been a word spoken louder or livelier than was seemly.

'*Well*, young people,' said he, in a tone that showed he thought it anything but well; 'what means this laughing and rejoicing that I hear? Are the concerns of our Church and nation so prosperous as to warrant idle tattling and mirth?'

We drew to one side; and Rosa, with a gesture more expressive than any speech, pointed to her brother.

'Captain Browning returned safe and well!' my father continued. 'I am truly glad, sir, to see you!' And here he shook hands with the newcomer warmly enough. 'But I know not why your return should cause these giddy-pates to fill my house with uproar.'

I was vexed beyond what I could bear in silence at being rated for a joy so very natural, as well as for a fault which we had not committed.

'Why, sir,' said I—and, sure, I knew while I made it that my protest was both foolish and useless—'would you have us take the mercies of God unthankfully? I believe you're still ignorant that Mr. Browning brings the news of Captain Hamilton's speedy return.'

'Does he so?' rejoined my father, with a manner I thought severer than before. 'And if he does, what then? Were it not more seemly, and liker your nurture, too, that you should go into your chamber, and there thank God upon your knees for His mercies, than to go beside yourself with gladness because you have good news? Good news, forsooth! I count them but ill news, if they cause you to behave yourself like those unregenerate fools without there in the Diamond.'

'Twas the noise in the Diamond, I make no doubt, that he had heard, and imputed it to us. And yet it was a chastened noise enough—the sounds of sober people rejoicing in all sobriety

as they escorted their friends to their homes.   I
could not forbear a glance at Rosa.   Alas! it
was a glance that said more than was safe in
the presence of one that had returned to the.
room unnoticed.

'Pray, young mistress,' broke in Mr. Hewson's grating voice, bitter with censure, 'answer
me one question : Are you afraid of the judg-
ments of Heaven or no ?   Is that your way of
receiving your father's weighty rebuke—well
merited as you must know it, in your heart—
with a sneer—a sneer addressed, too, to one
whom you would fain pervert from her
obedience? · Nay, deny it not ; I have marked
it too often.'

'You are mistaken, sir,' said I, as calmly as I
could, for this browbeating did cause the angry
colour to flame into my cheeks ; and my voice
betrayed too much of what I felt, for all my
governance.   'Nothing was further from my
wish than to sneer at anything my father said
to me.   I did but put to Rosa with my eyes
a question that I put to him with my lips a
moment before—to wit, Are we to see God
merely in His stripes, and not in His kindness ?
And, sir, I desire not to be uncivil to you, but
you are none of my father; and I think your
office scarce entitles you to rebuke one that is no
longer a member of your flock.'

Good lack! the fire-brand I had cast with these few words, which certainly I had done well to repress! There was no way to appease ·my father's anger, but to make full submission to his minister; and that I had so little stomach for, that I had preferred to quit his house, save for the grief it had been to my brother and sister. 'Twas their persuasion that brought Mr. Hewson to accept the very limited apology I forced myself to make, which was that, for what I had said amiss in my answer to him, I craved his pardon.

'But I beg you, of your courtesy, to understand, sir,' I said to him, speaking with the most extreme gentleness I could compass, 'that I cannot continue your pupil in spiritual matters. I should do you no credit, Master Hewson, nor —believe it, I pray you—would you do me any good. Each of us must follow the guidance of his own conscience. You would not, I am sure, have me do otherwise.' And with that I extended my hand to him.

A little to my surprise, he took it.

''Tis the old spirit, Mrs. Mary,' said he— 'the spirit I have grieved so oft to discern in you; the spirit of self-sufficiency, of pride, of rebellion. Well, Heaven hath its own modes of dealing with such faults. You have referred yourself to God's judgment; and if He punish

not—ay, speedily and sharply—this your over-
confidence—ay, and the idolatry of the creature
that led to your display of it—then are my inter-
pretations of His doings as far mistaken as you
think them.'

It was all but a curse; yet somehow the
man's manner, which had softened marvellously
after my declaration of independence, converted
it from that into a warning.   But at the evening
holding-forth, which followed anon (Captain
Browning waiting all the while for his supper),
this my rebellion, as he then phrased it, was so
handled that I thought Heaven had picked out,
already, a weapon to chastise me withal, and
a severe one, too.

But yet there was a kind of peace patched up
between us, and I thought sometimes thereafter
that I understood Mr. Hewson, and he me,
better than we had ever done before, for so long
as we had known each other.

CHAPTER XXII.

A BITTER DISAPPOINTMENT.

If the Ides of March were Cæsar's black day, whereon he could look for nothing but evil, 'tis sure the 21st of the same month that is mine. For on that day I received the sorest disappointment that ever I abode. Ay, for all that hath come and gone since then, I rate it still as the sorest and the bitterest.

That I was up with the first streak of day on the morning after Captain Browning's return, sure, it scarce needs telling; any that hath ever awaited a dear friend, and known him at the door, so to speak, would divine as much. Up I was and out, though the streets were quiet still, and empty; so empty and so quiet that the steps of the watch patrolling them could be heard at a great distance. I went upon the wall at the bastion at Butcher's Gate. Thence I had the view of the river that was denied me from mine own windows; and on the river, sure enough,

was that I had come out to see. There came
the ship, white-sailed and stately in the spreading light; for 'twas a lovely morning. She was
half-way between Culmore and the town by the
time I saw her, and the spring breeze sent her
bravely forward. 'Why,' thought I to myself,
'she will be safe at anchor before breakfast-
time. Who knows but Captain Hamilton may
breakfast this morning at his own table?
Why, scarcely,' I admonished myself considerately; 'he hath his command to look to.' But
yet the thought sent me home right speedily, to
make sure of good entertainment for him, if by
happy chance he should come so early.

That he did not was scarce a blemish on my
expectancy, for I had thought it but barely
possible; but I looked for him assuredly long
before dinner, and would not stir from the house,
lest he should arrive in my absence. But
dinner-time came and passed, and no James.
And then my hopefulness began to merge in
something that was hardly disquietude as yet,
but was wonder with a dash of bitterness in it—
a little discomfortable to sit at home and muse
upon.

Unwilling, therefore, to sit at home and muse,
I took my little son in my hand (pleasing myself
with the thought of the pleasure his father
would take in seeing him so sturdy and rosy),

and made my way to the quay. Margery
attended us, for appearances must be kept up
by daylight, howsoever glad surprise may
thrust them out of sight at dusk. I smiled to
myself, as we paced across the Diamond and
down Silver Street, to think how we had
traversed them the evening before, to say
nothing of my expedition of that very morning.

The quay was so thronged that I hesitated
at first to venture on it. My ship—the ship
from England—lay not alongside of it, but was
moored in the river a little distance from the
shore. But the *Mountjoy* was moored at the
quay, with half a dozen gangways between her
deck and the shore ; and, Lord ! what a turmoil
of unloading was going on ! Half the town, I
verily thought, was there receiving and carrying away their goods. And on the deck, nigh
to the mast, stood Captain Browning, sword in
hand, as I had seen him the evening before,
pointing and directing therewith as need arose.
'Twas a gesture that remained upon my mind
as native to him and characteristic.

He saw me at once, and came towards me.

' Well, Mrs. Hamilton,' said he, ' how is the
Captain, and hath he gone aboard his ship
again ?'

' You know at least as much about it as I do,'
I replied, feeling all of a sudden aggrieved and

slighted. 'He hath not yet found time to come into the town ; doubtless you have seen him ; I have not.'

I tried to make as though I jested, but knew it was a poor pretence that could deceive no one. Captain Browning, who had lifted Roland in his arms, set him down again ; methought he had a look upon his face that was something anxious, yet he spoke cheerily.

'To be sure,' said he ; 'and I might have known it without asking had I not been so full of mine own business. He hath a great trust committed to his care by the Government, and may not leave it, of course, till he can give it over to the person 'tis designed for. Perhaps, Mrs. Hamilton, you would like to go aboard of the *Jersey* frigate yourself? I'll set you across in my boat in a moment, and go with you myself if you'd like my escort.'

Had I had any desire to accept this offer, whereto the hindrances were more than the temptations, I had been prevented, for even as I opened my mouth to thank him for his kindness, there was a stir in the crowd behind us, and a cry that passed from mouth to mouth, 'The Governor—room for the Governor!'

Sure enough, across the space between the gate and the quay came Lundy, attended by some of the chief men of the city and county ;

Sir Arthur Rawdon and Colonel Stewart were
two of them. They looked, as I thought, both
wearied and out of heart, and well might they
be both. Lundy, having his attention drawn to
me, stopped and spoke.

'So, Mrs. Hamilton, you are here !' said he,
making a leg. And at that the rest that were
of mine acquaintance stepped forward, so that
there was a small buzz of greeting. 'I suppose,' Lundy resumed, when that was over,
'that you've been hearing, like the rest of us, of
your husband's return, with the Lord knows
what munitions of war.'

At that Sir Arthur took up the word, his
nostrils dilating suddenly like those of a restive
horse.

'The Lord knows our need of them,' said he.
''Tis the best mercy He hath sent us this
month ; sure am I of that.'

Lundy turned to me with a light laugh.

'Heard you ever such a pother about powder
and ball as these, our valiant defenders, make ?'
said he to me. 'One might think, to hear
them, that we of Derry had the whole of
Ireland to stand up for.'

'And have we not ?' I asked, sorry in my
heart that he had given such a turn to the talk,
with these gentlemen standing by, who were
many of them fresh from the disaster at

Dromore, and the rest, no doubt, fresh from failure at some other place.

At my question Sir Arthur flashed out with his answer, the 'Cock of the North' once more.

'Faith and indeed, madam! you're right,' said he to me. 'And faith and indeed, sir!' he repeated, turning to Lundy, ' it's a pretty pother we are put into when we want these same munitions of war and can get none. Had I but had powder enough, and ball sizeable to my arms, last week, it's a different account my brave fellows would have given of Richard Hamilton's.'

Colonel Lundy was visibly disconcerted. Instead of replying to Sir Arthur, whose face was all in a flame as he spoke, he turned round to Captain Browning, that stood by my side.

Most of the gentlemen had greeted him as an old acquaintance, but up till this moment Colonel Lundy had taken no manner of notice of him.

'You, sir, whatever your name is,' said he angrily, 'why keep you such a bustle of unloading here on the quay ? Can't it wait ?'

My blood boiled up at his arrogance.

'Sir,' I said to him, 'I pray you to know Captain Browning, a kinsman of mine and Captain Hamilton's. I have already had the honour to present him to you in mine own house—twice, I think.'

Colonel Lundy was off his high horse so very speedily that it almost seemed he had come by a fall.

'I beg the gentleman's pardon and yours, I'm sure, for my lack of recollection,' said he, in a very altered tone. 'But that hath nothing to do with the question I asked, which is—To what purpose is Captain Browning in so great haste to unload that my barge hath no room to approach?'

'I'd be grieved to interfere with your convenience, sir,' said Mr. Browning very quietly, 'or with the convenience of anyone else, for the matter of that. As to your barge, I think you'll find her awaiting you at the steps.'

Where, sure enough, she lay, and had lain for some minutes.

'When I can get at her, sir,' said Lundy peevishly. ''Tis the quay, and not the water, that you obstruct in your unseemly haste.'

Mr. Browning looked at him full and gravely, whereat the other dropped his eyes.

'I was about to observe, Colonel Lundy,' said he, 'that I see not how any haste can be too great when the enemy may be upon us any day, and Derry may have a siege to stand before we are many weeks older.'

'And that's very well said, sir,' remarked
Sir Arthur Rawdon in a low voice, and keeping
his eyes upon Lundy's face.

'A siege, sir!' said he, more peevishly than
before. 'I marvel to hear you. Is Derry a
town that could stand one, do you think?' At
that some of those that were in his company
cast very marked glances upon each other.
Lundy, I thought, perceived them. 'Suppose
she does,' he resumed, after a moment's silence,
'what are ye afraid of? Are you aware that
our storehouses are full of provision—full, I tell
you? You may even unload at your leisure,
sir; we could not at present bestow another
shipload of victual if we had it.'

'The next, sir,' said Mr. Browning, with
meaning emphasis, 'shall be mine own private
venture, and it will be mine own private loss if
it should go to waste.'

Lundy tried to draw down his brows, but
there was that in Mr. Browning's regard which
would not be overborne, and the frown wherewith he meant to confound us changed into a
scowl something wanting in dignity. He
muttered something under his breath, and
passed on to his barge without a word of
leave-taking, so that the other gentlemen
were forced to make theirs of the shortest.
We stood gazing after them in silence, hearing

his voice once or twice, but neither the words he spoke nor the answers he received, till, just as they put off from the steps, Colonel Stewart's voice sounded out clearly :

'Indeed, sir, since you will ask me, I think he was in the right.'

Then Captain Browning turned to me, his eyes like live coals.

'What thought you of that ?' said he. 'Why, 'tis treason,' he continued, his indignation getting the better of his composure—'flat treason, if ever the mouth of man spoke it !—treason ; he proclaimed it of himself. Heard you ever the like—to discourage the bringing of victual to the town at such a time ? Holloa, men there ! Work your hardest, lest the Governor lay an embargo on us before we get out our goods. Mrs. Hamilton, is the man a fool merely, think you, or the traitor he seems ?'

'Are you astonished ?' I asked of him, passing by the question. For the contrast between the men brought back to my mind the first time I had seen them in company together ; Lundy had betrayed his true character then, though later his craft had gone nigh to make me hate myself for that I had seen, and contemn mine own eyes for their seeing.

'You have suspected him from the first ?' said Captain Browning, in answer to my question.

'At times,' I answered. 'The man is so
finished a hypocrite that very often I have
blamed myself for suspicions that now I wish
I had spoken out. But strive as I might, I
could never fully trust him.'

'I wish the rest of us had been as clear of
sight,' said he ruefully.

'I wish,' I rejoined, 'that there be eyes
enough opened even now to do any good.'

It was plain that my presence on the quay
saw doing none, but the contrary ; and so I took
my leave of him, and returned to my house,
there to await my husband's leisure with what
patience I could muster.

And I had need of all I could muster, truly,
for the afternoon passed into evening, and the
evening was falling dusk before there came a
soul to my door.

Meanwhile the streets of the town were full
of a growing stir ; it was plain there was news
abroad, for with every minute there came more
people out of the houses to join those that were
already talking in little groups at the doors and
at the corners. And that it was good news
was as evident, for every face beamed with
satisfaction. It seemed truly as if that ship
from England had brought over a cargo of
happiness as well as of powder and lead, and
methought that every soul in Derry was to

have his ration thereof before my turn should
come.

Snatches of the talk came to mine ears as I
sat and watched the growing crowd. 'The
Prince,' 'The King,' and 'The Proclamation'
were words that mingled with those I was
prepared for—to wit, 'powder' and 'money'
and 'stand of arms.' But the sounds of passing feet and of cheerful voices, broken now
and then with distant shouts, though blending
the whole into one noise, defrauded the parts
of any trace of meaning. My curiosity grew
with the growing crowd, till it came to so great
a height that I believe I clean forgot mine own
private impatience.

I had presently sent Margery out to gather
tidings, but when the gathering of tidings was
in question, 'twas usually hardly needful to
send her. So it proved in this case, for she
came at the first sound of my silver call with
'great tidings' writ plain upon every inch of
her face, so that I could not forbear to smile.

'What is it?' I asked her. 'It's very plain
you know.'

'Madam,' said she, half out of breath with
her own eagerness, 'I scarce know where to
begin ; there's so much to tell, and all so good.
Derry's a made town, though the whole of
Ireland should come against it, for there's near

five hundred barrels of powder brought over in
the English ship, besides I know not how many
stand of arms—some say a thousand; and
money—faith, I scarce know what's the use of
it when we have all it can buy without it; but,
anyhow, there's money in plenty, besides the
arms.'

'Why, this is excellent hearing!' said I, with
satisfaction tingling through my veins like
wine, for was not this Captain Hamilton's
doing? 'Now I understand the cheery faces
and voices there without in the streets.'

'You'll understand them better when you've
heard the whole of the news,' quoth Margery;
'for that's the least of it.'

'Make haste with the rest, then!' said I
sharply. 'If that's the least of it, what, for all
sakes, is the best?'

'The news of the King is sure the best,'
said Margery, with a little curtsey as she said
the word 'King,' such as the Catholics use to
make at the mention of the Holy Name in the
Creed.

I was nothing enlightened, but only puzzled.

'What of the King?' I asked her. 'There's
a rumour that he hath landed at Kinsale; but
that's no matter for joy, but the contrary;
unless, to be sure, he hath ceded the kingdom
to the Prince of Orange, as he was advised.'

'Then, that's what he hath done, no doubt,' said Margery. 'For the Prince of Orange is Prince of Orange no longer, but King of England.'

'That's an old, old story,' I interrupted her impatiently. 'He's King of England, sure enough, but what is he here?'

'Why, I know not what he is to-night,' said Margery; 'but he'll be King here likewise to-morrow morning. For the great news is that King William and Queen Mary are to be proclaimed to-morrow at noon in the Diamond; 'tis that that hath sent the people wild with joy. Do but listen.'

Truly, now that I knew what they were shouting for, I could distinguish the words well enough. 'God save the King!' that was the burden of them; 'God save King William and Queen Mary!' 'God save the King and Queen!'

'That's glorious news indeed!' said I joyfully.

'Is it daddy come home?' asked little Roland, who had been gazing from one to the other of us all this time with a puzzled face.

I hesitated, scarce knowing what reply to make to the child's question. But Margery answered it straight, and so simply that all my

doubts and fears cleared away like mist before
the sun.

'Why,' said she, 'the master must sure be
at the very door by this time. They tell me
he couldn't leave the ship till the Governor
came to take possession of the gunnery and
treasure, and the rumour goes that Colonel
Lundy hath taken the oaths to William and
Mary already on board of the frigate.'

'He'd have to, I should think,' said I, 'on
purpose to qualify himself to receive the
stores.'

'No doubt,' rejoined Margery. 'And,
madam, every man that passes the news to
his neighbours adds this, by way of conclusion:
"How well hath Captain Hamilton deserved
of the town for his prosperous discharge of his
errand!"'

I broke into joyous laughter.

'I can't forbear to admire your talent for
news-telling, Margery,' I told her, 'and the
art wherewith you contrived to keep back the
best of the news till the last.'

For was it not the best of the news for me?
—to know that he had discharged his errand
with credit to himself and to the satisfaction of
everyone concerned. Straight, as if the waiting were over, indeed, the moment I knew the
cause of it, came the knock upon the door I

had been listening for so long. Margery ran
to open it; I, withheld by I know not what
instinct, stood still where I was. But Roland
ran with Margery to meet his father at the
door.

With the sound of its opening I was assured
of something amiss; a kind of shudder passed
through me from head to foot. Angered at
myself for what I took to be mere folly—a
freak of the nerves worthy of some spoilt fine
lady—I stepped to the door of the room,
wondering a little vaguely why there was no
babble of greeting without, but instead of it a
kind of hush that meant—— What did it
mean?

What it meant I could not see for the dusk
that had fallen unnoticed while I was talking
with Margery. But I heard, and that was as
much as I needed. Strange—that joy must
needs be witnessed to by every sense we have,
but any one of them gives sufficient certitude
of the reality of pain.

The voice that I heard was none of Captain
Hamilton's, and though it struck on mine ear
familiarly, I could not remember whose it was.
But in another moment its owner was in the
room beside me. There was more light there
than in the passage—enough to see his features.
I recognised my visitor in one moment, and

with an exclamation of relief. For it was my husband's cousin, James Hamilton also by name—Captain James Hamilton, son to my Lady Hamilton, my husband's aunt. There was nothing in his aspect that bespoke him the bearer of ill tidings.

'You seem astonished to see me, cousin,' said he.

'I am,' said I. 'It was James that I expected. I suppose you come as his envoy?'

'Why, yes,' said he, 'you may put it that way. I bring you a letter from him.'

'A letter!' I said, amazed. 'Will he not be here to-night, then?'

'Why, hardly,' said he. His voice began to have a tone of concern in it. 'Sure,' continued he, 'you haven't been all this time in the belief that it was he that was come over in the *Jersey* frigate from England!'

'How could I think otherwise?' said I. 'Was it not he that was entrusted with the errand? Is it not natural enough that he should return with the thing he went for?'

James Hamilton stood for a moment perfectly silent.

'It was,' he replied presently, speaking slowly. 'It was natural you should expect him instead of me—quite natural. All I wish is that I had thought of it sooner; you should

have had your letter in the morning by another
hand.'

'Even now,' I said to him, 'I suppose I must
be stupefied; but I scarce seem able to comprehend how you come to be put in his place.'

'It's simple enough,' says he, 'if you will
but think so. One James Hamilton—that's he
—was despatched in quest of necessaries of
war; he went, and he procured them. But
another James Hamilton hath actually brought
them over; that's I, cousin, and here I am.'

'You say that he went and he procured
them,' said I, trying to make the thing clear to
mine own mind. 'Why, then, hath he trans-
ferred his trust to you? Hath any harm be-
fallen him?'

'None whatever, that I know of,' said he.
'Won't you read your letter, cousin?'

'I beg you will explain it to me,' said I; for
so dazed did I feel, that I doubted whether
written characters would have any meaning to
my eyes.

'Why, briefly, then, 'tis this,' said he; and I
could see he was something ill at ease. 'James
arrived in England about the same time as
Baldwin Leighton; like him, he was admitted
to the presence of all the heads of the Protestant
party—to Shrewsbury's, to the presence of the
King himself, I was given to understand. Like

Leighton's, his mission was perfectly successful; 'twas he, as I told you a minute ago, who procured the supplies that I have brought over. All of a sudden he hears in the midst of his business that a friend of his, my Lord Mountjoy, is cast into the Bastile in France upon a charge of some ancient treason to King James, which Hamilton took it into his head he could clear him of. After that—well, you know him, cousin, if anyone doth. He had but one thought in his head, and that was to make the speediest of his way to Paris, to the succour of his friend. I was at hand. I bore the same name as his own. I was his kinsman, and he knew me fit to discharge his trust. So he got it made over to me, and here I am, having, I hope, done nothing to discredit his confidence.'

'A moment!' said I. One expression he had used had taken my ear, and I felt that 'twas a matter of life and death to me to know everything. 'You said,' I continued, 'that you bore the same name as my husband. What had that to do with your acceptance of his trust?'

'Why, everything,' said he; but he reddened, and, in spite of the dusk, I perceived it. 'The commission was made out to Captain James Hamilton, and 'tis Captain James Hamilton that hath discharged it. Where's the fault in that?'

'But let me understand,' said I. 'I pray

you patience. I know I am dull to very blank-
ness to-night. For you couldn't, I am sure,
have taken James's commission, even though
the names were the same, without the leave of
the authority he had it from.'

'Gad so l' said he, rather blankly. 'Perhaps we acted rashly, but that's exactly what
we did. "Captain James Hamilton" was all
the name that was named—no further designa-
tion of any kind. You see, he had been broke.
Why should we have troubled Shrewsbury,
when there was not so much as a letter to be
altered ?'

I found myself laughing as he finished.
Certes, 'twas with anything else than mirth.

'Then 'tis desertion he is guilty of, neither
more nor less,' said I. ''Tis disgrace he hath
earned by this business, and not credit.'

'Never name it, cousin,' said he earnestly.
'Who is to know it but ourselves, if we keep
our own counsel ?'

'You, cousin,' said I, 'are right enough ; you
have done the thing you undertook. King
William hath nothing to say to you, that I can
see, but thanks. Nay '—for he flew into a
passion of protesting—'I know it was not of
that you were thinking. You meant to act the
part of a true friend, and no doubt, to his mind,
you've done it. But all the same, he hath

earned himself disgrace, and nothing else—disgrace, and not credit.'

' I know not why you will say so,' said he. ' Not a soul suspects but 'twas I was the right holder of the commission.'

' There's not a soul in Derry,' said I, ' but knows it was he that went for the supplies.'

' Ah !' said he, ' but not one of them took it into his head to doubt me—not one. They are satisfied, and never a word will you hear about the matter, if you will but keep your own counsel, as I told you.'

' It may be so,' said I. ' Well, you have shielded his name, cousin, and for that I thank you. But for all that, in your mind, and in mine, and in his own, I nothing doubt, by this time, James Hamilton is a man that hath deserted his trust, and hath deserved, not disgrace merely——'

I stopped, unwilling to name the further penalty.

' Faith and indeed, I'm as bad as he is !' said our cousin; 'for, I assure ye, I saw no harm in it.'

He took his leave with these words, leaving me with my disappointment to bear, and my child to comfort, and my letter to read.

But was I not right, when I set down, in the beginning of the story of this day, that it saw the bitterest disappointment of all my life ?

CHAPTER XXIII.

TELLS HOW A CHANGE OF SOVEREIGNS WAS EFFECTED.

To comfort the child was no easy task; for he was near heart-broken to hear that his father was neither returned nor likely to return. But sleep, that is the mightiest consoler in the world, came to the help of my poor efforts; and by-and-by I laid his little tear-flushed face upon the pillow, his sorrow all forgot. Then I took out my letter to read it; the first letter from Captain Hamilton I had ever laid by to wait my leisure. Now that my leisure served, I was in no great hurry to break the seal. I turned it over in my hand with a shrinking feeling, as though it were a living thing and hurtful. But at last I opened it and read it.

It gave nearly word for word the same tale as his cousin had told me an hour before; together with such endearments as could not fail to soothe mine indignation, while they did but add new keenness to my grief. I could but

marvel how a man that was so keen upon the
point of honour could have stepped so far
astray. For the whole compulsion was in that
point of honour; my lord, he said, was called
in question for his leniency to him; 'twas his
part, especially as he had so grievously mis-
understood and wronged him, to see him fully
cleared. Over and over again I read one
sentence that a little showed his mind.

'Mine errand,' so he wrote, 'suffers no detri-
ment; for my cousin hath the cause at heart as
truly as I, and will venture himself as frankly
for its sake as I could do.'

Sometimes I thought this to appear some
excuse for him; then presently it seemed none
at all; at last mine angry grief had the upper
hand, so that I tore the letter into little pieces
and cast it to the winds. The happier I, had I
been able to cast away with it the thought of
my husband's error.

All the world knows of our proclamation of
King William and Queen Mary the next day.
Our good Bishop, that went to Raphoe in a pet
at our resistance to the Right Divine, on the
7th of December last, was present and helped
to transfer the Right Divine to a different
holder. After that I suppose that his conscience and his will led him in the same straight
road. A humbler individual was present like-

wise ; to wit, Mrs. Hamilton of Cloncally, in
whose ears the triumphing and rejoicing were
at first something of the flattest, though for fear
of grieving her friends (and in part, perhaps,
from a less worthy reason) she owned it not.
After a time even her moping mood became
infected by the general joy ; sure, it were a
heart both sullen and selfish that could nurse
its own pain amid the national rejoicing for a
national deliverance. This was nothing less,
though we garnered not its fruits so soon as we
hoped.

After the proclamation, there arose a curious
hitch in the proceedings. All the officers, both
civil and military, were required to take the
oaths to the new sovereigns, before they should
receive their commissions in their names. Now,
by rights, the very first to take these oaths
should have been our worshipful Governor,
Colonel Lundy ; but Colonel Lundy took them
not at all, that I could see, though he read his
commission, and seemed very active in helping
to swear the rest. The people were not slow
to notice the omission, and soon there arose a
clamour that the Governor had not sworn, and
that the Governor must take the oaths like
other folk. He answered them at some length ;
but only a word or two of what he said reached
our ears ; the people appeared still dissatisfied.

After that he spoke to them again, appealing to
Captain Hamilton, who stood beside him on
the platform ; it seemed that he confirmed what
the Governor had said, and then the people
were silenced. But one or two of those that
were near the Governor were seen to expostu-
late with him. We wondered what the difficulty should be. After a time Wamphray came
to us, and we asked him what it was. A small
matter, he told us—merely that Lundy objected
to taking the oaths twice over.

'He says,' said Wamphray, 'that he took
them in Hamilton's cabin aboard of the *Jersey* ;
and 'tis certain that he hath helped to swear the
rest, which is a decided step enough !'

'Why, there are others here besides he that
were aboard the *Jersey* last night,' said I. 'And
they have taken the oaths this morning. Here
comes one of them'—it was Sir Arthur Rawdon
—'let us ask him about it.'

But 'twas impossible to ask questions of Sir
Arthur until we had answered his ; which were
a consolation to me, as showing by their tone
that what our cousin had told me the day before
was perfect truth ; I mean, that no soul he had
spoken to had suspected that he was but his
kinsman's substitute, and a substitute unsanc-
tioned by the authorities. Afterward he was
ready enough to describe what had happened.

As soon as they were gone aboard of the
Jersey, Captain Hamilton received them and
showed them his letter of instructions, satisfying
them, so he said, that he was the right commissioner. Lundy then immediately desired a
private interview with him.

'And faith, Mrs. Hamilton,' said Sir Arthur,
I was very near coming ashore to tell you we
were all in error about the envoy; but I could no
longer spy you on the quay; perhaps also I had
no great liking for the errand, for who desires
to be the bearer of unwelcome news? By-and-
by, when Beverley and the rest of us had pretty
well worn out our patience, Hamilton and Lundy
came on deck together; and Lundy told us that
he had taken the oaths to William and Mary,
which Hamilton confirmed.'

'But why,' one of us inquired, 'should that
prevent him from taking them again to-day,
since it would be so great a satisfaction to the
whole city?'

'He hath an objection to swearing twice,'
said Sir Arthur, 'as if, alone among all of us,
swearing once were not enough to bind him.'

'But you?' said Wamphray. 'Sure, I saw
you take them half an hour ago. Were you
not sworn yesterday as well as he?'

'Not I, young gentleman,' said the other.
'Faith, I obeyed the Bible precept yesterday,

and swore not at all. If you ask the reason, it is that the thing was never named to me. Lundy, I suppose, in a sudden passion of loyalty at the sight of his commission, went down on his knees incontinent, and would not be withholden.'

'There are a few of us,' said Wamphray, 'that would fain have had the evidence of our own eyes and ears to that. Perhaps you haven't observed it, but there's a doubtful ring about him now and then that's a bar to perfect confidence.'

'I won't conceal from you,' replied Sir Arthur, 'that there have been times when I've gone very near to sharing the feeling. Did you hear of the scene at Coleraine the other day? You have? Then you know that it's pretty widely spread in certain quarters. But it would appear as though 'twere merely circumstances that deceived us. There should be no doubt about his mind after his conduct to-day.'

'He hath been very active, that's certain,' said Wamphray. 'But, to my mind, 'tis an enthusiasm that hath been a little over-sudden in coming on.'

'Why, man, have you no use of your fancy?' said the other, laughing. 'I say not that his mind hath never wavered. On the contrary, I think it hath; this very sudden rapture's the

proof.   But can't you figure to yourself the
relief of settling a wavering mind ? like steady-
ing a palsied hand.   The man will be ten
times more of an enthusiast now than the
righteous from the beginning that needed no
repentance.   And now,' he resumed presently,
'I must even take my leave of you and get me
gone.'

'That's sudden,' said I.   'It must be pressing
business, sure, that calls you from Derry to-day.
Can't you stay and feast with the rest of the
loyal folk ?'

'I wish I could, indeed,' said he.   'But it
would argue small loyalty on my part if I did.
A man must even do his work before he
snatches his pleasure.   Coleraine's in nothing
like so prosperous a case as Derry, and I am
needed there, for all so humble a creature as I
am.   The news of this day's doings will be as
good as a thousand men to them,' said he,
making a movement as if he would have leapt
for joy.   And so took his leave indeed, and
turned to go, but in a moment was again by
Wamphray's side.   'I would not,' said he im-
pressively, 'nourish suspicions of any man's
disposition that are founded on what is past and
gone, much less of a general's.   Why, a general,
if he have any talent, is bound to have his secret
plans and projects, which if declared are frus-

trate at once. Why, man, don't I know it by
myself? 'Tis the very mark of your raw
undrilled men that they will still be trying to
thrust themselves into the councils of their
officers.'

' Meaning Lundy by the General, and myself
by the raw undrilled recruit?' asked Wamphray,
laughing.

' No offence, I hope?' said Sir Arthur.

' None in the world,' said Wamphray, 'save
that I can't help thinking that a man should
show something of generalship, if he desires
confidence like that you speak of.'

' No doubt,' said the other. ' But yet, luck's
a lottery, and 'tis no more than decent to give
him a fair chance.'

After that he got himself gone in good
earnest. The good news from England had
been a very medicine to him; he looked
another man than the Sir Arthur that had
spoken to me on the ship-quay the evening
before. The old fire was in his eye, the old life
in his steps. It was the old Sir Arthur, ready
to make of hardship a jest, and of defeat a
stepping-stone to victory, that left us that day
in the Diamond of Derry.

Could I but show the likeness of the same
man as we saw him next, less than three
weeks after, 'twere a livelier picture of what

had passed in the meantime than if I should take every day separately and describe its sufferings from dawn to dawn ; for night brought neither rest nor refreshment to the watchers of the Bann. When two or three thousand men attempt the work of a great army, sure the best of everything should be placed at their service. Encouragement should be lavished on them; if supplies be in the country, they are entitled to the first of them. But in the case of our poor, gallant, ill-starred little army, the clean contrary was the treatment they met with. Half armed, and not half fed, nor nothing near it ; without shelter of any kind, save what the bare March trees and hedges afforded them ; so few, considering their task, that rest was totally out of the question—what could be expected but that they should fail ? Never was failure less inglorious ; but yet it was failure and not success, and the Catholic army effected the passage of the river in spite of all our men could do. Then, the stimulus of hope being withdrawn from their spirits, the hardships they had suffered took effect both on these and on their health. Many died ; many were so broken in health that to this day they have not recovered their strength. Sir Arthur Rawdon was no more than an example ; and he was like a walking corpse for ghastliness, and like an

infant for weakness, when he came back into
Derry after the passage of the Bann.

The next act in the tragedy was the evacua-
tion of Coleraine, and after that it seemed as
though the whole population of the county were
coming into Derry. To keep a house to one's
self was out of all question. I found that I
must either share mine or quit it. Either was
a grief; but when a thing has to be done, to
what purpose is it to delay or to murmur?
Two kind friends were equally willing to receive
me and my small family—Mrs. Browning and
my father. It were scarce the truth to say that
the advantages of both courses were almost
equally balanced; for, in truth, it was the dis-
advantages I found myself dwelling on, so
carping was my temper grown. But after much
consideration, it seemed, upon the whole, best
to be in my father's house in these troublesome
times, and there, in a mood so grudging that I
was even ashamed of it myself, I removed upon
the 7th of April; the rumours of the enemy's
approach being every day more instant, brought
in by the flying country-folk that took refuge in
the city.

Now was the punctual moment when a skilled
commander might have retrieved the fortune of
the war. Our outposts, as one might express
it, were all gone, taken by the enemy; Hills-

borough, Dungannon, Coleraine, the whole
course of the Bann—all were in their hands,
together with the stores that were accumulated
in the places of strength ; and that was bad for
us.   And it were idle to deny that our men had
this time lost heart, which perhaps was the
worst part of their ill-fortune.   But, on the
other hand, the whole strength of our army was
now concentrated in Derry ; the Fin was yet
between us and the enemy ; and if our men had
lost heart and health, they had gained both
experience and fortitude.   Any that doubts
that needs but to recall them as they came in
from Coleraine, every man bringing as much
victual as he and his horse could carry, and
having burnt all that he could not carry off, lest,
falling into Hamilton's hands, it might prove
help to him.

At this critical moment, what was Lundy's
conduct ?   To hearten those that were so sorely
in need of heartening ?   Nay, but to whisper
despair in their ears, and to shout it in the
public streets.   To encourage them that had
suffered both from hunger and exposure by the
sight of those stuffed store-houses he had
spoken of so lately ?   Nay, but to change his
tale from day to day, so that at one moment he
chides the new-comers for their useless pains in
bringing in supplies to a town already liberally

victualled for a year, and the next refuses these
very men admittance to that very town upon
the plea that so many mouths could not be
maintained for a fortnight.

Had he offered to lead them against the
enemy, sure the clamour of applause he had
raised had gone near to reach their ears. Had
he said, 'The Fin is now our frontier line of
defence; come, let me post you in the fittest
places while there's time to choose them unmolested,' he had retrieved the confidence of
the men, both in themselves and in him their
leader. Instead, he made it his business to
disperse them hither and thither, one regiment
to Lifford, and another to Strabane, and others
to I know not what places, whispering still
despair in the ears of them and of their officers
—despair and selfish prudence; so that these
men, who had already ventured themselves so
gallantly in their country's quarrel, began to
withdraw themselves in great numbers into
England and Scotland, and of those that remained, many turned their eyes thitherward,
waiting but good opportunity to follow their
example.

But at this moment, Providence having still
a care of us, two things happened that brought
into view the concern that was felt for us in
England: one was the return of our trusty

messenger David Cairns from thence, neither
empty-handed nor depressed, but bringing
tidings of ample succour already on the way
to us, men and munitions both. How, think
you, was he received by the men of Derry,
whose worth as soldiers their Governor rated so
meanly? Why, he could scarce make his way
through the streets to his house, so closely was
he surrounded by men hanging on his words,
as though they by themselves were salvation.
Many a man that began with shouting ended
with a womanish sob, so closely it pleased them
at the heart to have the means of warfare given
them; and that at the very moment when their
leader's tale was that they were trembling with
anxiety to make their peace.

The next morning there was so great a
shouting that it was like the proclaiming of the
King and Queen a second time. And what,
think you, was the cause of this tumult of joy?
'Twas a proclamation that was affixed to the
door of the Diamond House, signed by all the
principal men in the city, and it ran thus:

'We, the officers hereto subscribing, pursuant
to a resolution taken and agreed upon at a
Council of War at Londonderry held this day,
do hereby mutually promise and engage to
stand by each other against the common enemy;
and will not leave the kingdom, nor desert the

public service, until our affairs are in a settled
and secure posture. And if any of us shall do
the contrary, the person so leaving the kingdom,
or deserting the service, without consent of a
Council of War, is to be deemed a coward, and
disaffected to their Majesties' service and the
Protestant interest.'

This was signed by above a score of the most
prominent gentlemen in the place; and it was
wonderful to see the satisfaction it gave, as
assuring the people of the opportunity they
desired to measure themselves fairly with their
opponents.

CHAPTER XXIV.

THE WORST OF OUR ENEMIES.

BUT though articles of war and declarations of union might be drawn up and signed, it should seem that we were none the nearer to fighting. The heart of the city seethed like a boiling cauldron in its eagerness to be doing something; but nothing was found fit to be done by our General. On the contrary, he showed a marvellous great ingenuity in finding good reason why we should sit still and attempt nothing. The charger was full of mettle, and chafed against the bit; but, faith, the reins were in hands both strong and cunning. Chafe as we might, he kept us well in hand.

It came to a point at last, however, as was to be expected. On the 12th of April, when there ran a rumour through the city that the enemy's ships were in the Lough, 'twas the old story; the most excellent reasons were brought forward why nothing should be done against them. There was, indeed, but one ship in the river, Mr. Cairns's, the *Jersey* and the *Mountjoy* being both gone; 'to what purpose were it,' said the Governor in council, 'to venture one against a fleet? or why should we weaken ourselves by courting a certain defeat?' 'Twas the last straw. So passionate a clamour arose, not in the council-chamber alone, but in the very streets, that he was forced to give way; and leave being once granted to use the ship as a privateer, there was such a rush to man her as never was equalled by men in the extremity of terror flying for their lives. What these men ran to do, was to put theirs in jeopardy in defence of the cause their hearts were full of; and with such headlong eagerness did they throng upon the quay (there being little room in the ship, and every man desiring to be one in her crew) that some were even shouldered into the water in the crowd. The expedition came to nothing; for when our privateer came into the Lough there were no ships to be seen, the heavy wind that blew that day having driven them back. But though never a blow was struck, there was a sense of achievement felt in the town. Merely to have given a loose to the fighting spirit that was in them, and that had been so long thwarted and restrained, seemed a kind of victory, or at the least an augury of victory.

Next day we had our first sight of the enemy, and a mere passing glimpse it was. They came down to the Waterside, and having got one field-piece into position, fired one shot at us. There were eight sakers and twelve demi-culverins on the walls of Derry, but not a single round of ammunition did our gunners possess among them to return the enemy's salute; in truth, they scarce had the time if they had had the means. The Catholic forces did but show themselves, and then departed, marching up the river in the direction of Strabane; for without boats 'twas impossible to come at us across the Foyle.

The whole town drew, as one might figure it, a long breath of readiness. Now at last there was to be an end of delay, upon whatever plausible pretext it might be urged. And, in truth, before the enemy's backs were well turned, there was a tuck of drum sent through the streets, announcing a council of war to be held forthwith, to which, 'tis scarce needful to say, that every man with the smallest title or pretension to be present crowded in, so that many had to be asked to retire to make room for those whose opinions were desired.

'Twas now the afternoon of Saturday; the

enemy were upon their way to the fords of Fin, for we had seen them. Could we make haste too great to be there before them, think you? I scarce can credit mine own recollection when I remember that the hour agreed upon for the rendezvous was ten of the clock o' Monday morning. That Lundy should have proposed it is easy enough to understand, in the light of what he had done before and what he afterwards did. But that the rest should have submitted their judgment to his is more than anyone can now account for or almost confess to.

To us women in the house it seemed clean incredible. With mounted messengers galloping out of all the landward gates—to Adam Murray at Culmore; to Major Crofton at Lifford; to my Lord Kingston at Ballyshannon, where not? — it should seem as there were really an earnest readiness to be on the ground. But *Monday morning at ten of the clock!* What was the enemy to be doing in the meantime, or what should hinder them to march the poor fourteen miles to Claudy Ford, there to effect their crossing in all leisure and safety before ever a man of ours should be on the ground to do so much as forbid them?

Not a man but left the council-chamber mur-

muring and dissatisfied, yet nothing is more
certain than that they altogether submitted
themselves to Lundy's will. It should seem
almost as though he possessed a spell wherewith to compel their assent to that which their
better judgment condemned and could not but
condemn.

The one only reason that was assigned in my
hearing for a compliance so extraordinary was
that it was necessary to give time for my Lord
Kingston and others of our friends (that should
have been posted a week before at the very
places they were now to hasten to) to join us at
Long-causey or at Claudy Ford. Sure, that
reason contradicted itself in the very statement. An hundred resolute men on the ground
are better, sure, than a thousand that are only
on their way to it. And 'twas an impossibility
on the face of it for the notice to reach my Lord
Kingston at Ballyshannon, and he to conduct
his troops to Claudy Ford between the evening
of Saturday and *Monday morning at ten of the
clock.*

I do think that there was in the whole of
Derry but one man that sympathized with
Lundy's action or would have defended it, and
we discovered him by a curious chance. Our
house was thrown, 'tis scarce needful to relate,
into a mighty bustle of preparation, for Wam-

phray was to ride to Culmore immediately, with
every man he could muster, to join Adam
Murray, under whom he was enrolled. The
men were few enough—three besides himself
and no more—for the successive enlistments
had drained away both my father's servants and
my own. But even so, there was much to be
done for them and few hands to do it, our
retinue of maidservants being near as shrunken
as our tale of men.

Rosa and I and Margery (who in my father's
house was promoted to be Mistress Margery,
and set over the other maids) thought it no
derogation to set our hands to the work in the
scarcity of other service. The time passed
quicker than we were aware of, and behold!
we were found to be trenching on the hours of
the Sabbath rest, as Master Hewson counts
them, not being ready to appear at the evening
exercise at the usual time. He had the presumption to come himself to summon us thereto ;
and finding us disposed to finish the work we
had in hand before we commenced our devo-
tions, expressed his displeasure, as usual, by
attributing it to the Divine mind.

'God could not,' he told us, 'bless an under-
taking that was begun by an infringement of His
law.' And then went on to prophesy defeat and
every kind of disaster to us at great length.

As usual, the man's arrogance and harshness became more than I could endure, and I found myself giving him a sharp answer.

'You are over-fond, sir, it seems to me,' said I, 'of deciding what the Almighty can and cannot do. Being Almighty, sure 'tis open to make use of us as His weapons, for all so unworthy as we be.'

At that he changed the direction of his denunciations, and began to pour them out upon me, which truly he might have done until he ceased from perfect weariness, for all I cared. But Margery could not endure to hear me so berated. Presently she put in her word, and then we found, and Master Hewson found, that he had met his match for once.

'It's ill pouring water on a drowned mouse, sir,' said she, burnishing briskly the while at Wamphray's harness. 'If the half of what you foretell to the whole country come to pass, my mistress will be destroyed with the rest of the nation; and I scarce see how anything more can happen to her after that.'

Upon that he began (willing to deprive me of my champion) to set forth my special transgressions, as he held them; but he was very speedily silenced.

'Hold your prating tongue, sir!' said she, her

indignation getting the upper hand of her
manners. 'Even in our women's ears such
folly rings false and hollow. Were the men to
hear you, they would never listen to you more,
even when you speak of things you understand.
What ! if the enemy appeared upon the Fords
of Fin on the Sabbath—as sure they will—
would you let them over rather than to profane
it by firing upon them ?'

'That would I verily,' said he, 'and beat
them upon Monday.'

'If they forbore till Monday to make an end
of you,' said she, with contempt in her voice
and in her face. 'Sure, there never was ranker
folly spoken in frenzy.'

Master Hewson, despairing to influence her,
actually turned away and relieved us of his
presence. Rosa and I were flippant enough to
make Margery our compliment of her victory.

'We must have you in the army directly,' we
said to her ; 'one that can rout Master Hewson
can certainly put to flight a whole regiment of
Tories.'

Perhaps she thought we were laughing at
her ; but assuredly Mistress Margery looked
not best pleased with our flattery.

Master Hewson might retire before an
adversary so callous to the pretensions of his
office, but he was not defeated ; to the contrary,

he executed a flank movement and had us all
on the hip ; for, our preparations being. finished,
and we able to appear at the exercise, he took
up the controversy (as his wont was when gain-
said) and pressed his views hard upon us, going
even so far as to render thanks to God that our
Governor was of so pious a temper, and so
resolved to preserve the sanctity of the Sabbath.
For once, however, he had reckoned without
his host, both literally and figuratively. Margery and we—I put Margery first, as she had
made herself our champion—found an unexpected ally in my father, who rated Mr. Hewson
soundly for his thanksgiving as soon as the
servants were gone from the room.   The dispute was hot for a few moments ; then Mr.
Hewson withdrew, silenced again, but still
unconquered, for he muttered, as one that
speaks to himself :

'The Lord *cannot* bless arms that are so
wielded, regardless of His law.'

' "*Cannot*" again,' said I aside to Rosa,
thinking myself unheard by him.

But he turned upon us fiercely.

'*Cannot*, young mistress—yes, *cannot*,' said
he, with bitter emphasis.   'We have high
authority for saying that God *cannot* be tempted
with evil.'

'We have equal authority for saying that

" the Sabbath was made for man, and not man for the Sabbath," ' said my father, with a mien of authority equal to his own. I gazed at him, surprised.

' I will even go and pray for you, sir,' said Mr. Hewson.

' Pray for sense, sir!' said my father sharply; much in the tone, indeed, in which he might have spoken to Wamphray, had they differed.

I drew Rosa aside, fearing lest we should smile, and be seen and rebuked; because it was an old question with us, often debated, whether, if a difference should arise between his minister and himself, Mr. Murray would assert his own opinion or yield to the authority of the other.

' I scarce think,' said Rosa very softly, but very merrily, ' that the last word hath been said yet in this dispute.'

There was little merriment either in her face or voice, however, an hour or two later, when we stood together in the doorway peering after Wamphray and his men, that were riding down the dusky street. The cressets glinted on their helmets and harness; and we could see them turn their heads for a farewell glimpse of us. Rosa leant upon my shoulder; and I knew there were tears on her cheek, though her face was turned away from me.

'Does one get hardened to these partings by custom, do you think?' said she. Her voice was a little unsteady.

'I doubt it,' I replied to her; and mine own was less clear than I could have wished. 'But, sure,' said I, a minute later—and there was a bitter quivering in mine that I would fain have hidden, but could not—'you would never wish to keep him at home at such a time?'

She lifted her head with a movement as though she would fain have looked me in the face; but the dark forbade that, and I was grateful.

'No,' said she—'oh no! that were baseness. That were a selfishness far more apt to anger God, and call down His vengeance upon us, than to prepare for their start on Saturday after sunset.'

We went into the house hand-in-hand, like children, and remained so, Rosa taking her turn of being comforter, for she had partly divined my grief, and I knew it, though neither of us so much as glanced at it in our talk. Whether it was a relief to me or a pang, to be thus understood, was more than I could tell. For mine was a sorrow that could not bear the light.

CHAPTER XXV.

THE RESULT OF HIS TREACHERY.

NEVER, I think, did the common every-day business of life seem so trivial as on the Monday morning. To balance hope and fear, weighing each against the other; to pour out the heart in prayer; to waste it in care that served no purpose; were the occupations in which we would have chosen to pass our time; while the battle that should determine life or death to many of us, freedom or slavery to all, was being fought out a few short miles away. That we were forced to bestir ourselves about common matters made little difference so far as our minds were concerned. At such moments the soul hath a life of its own, apart from the bodily; and every breath we draw is a prayer unspoken.

The scale wherein fear was poised outweighed the other, past all comparison, about ten of the clock. '*Ten of the clock, o' Monday*

morning '; 'twas the hour set for the muster at
Claudy Ford.   At that punctual minute—our
thoughts being there with our friends—our ears
were distracted by a heavy rumbling, that came
up from the streets below.   I know not why,
but it seemed a sound of ill augury, even when
we knew not its cause.   Judge if we thought it
less, or better, when we found that it was made
by the waggons of ammunition, which were
then, at the very time appointed for the meeting, only leaving the town.   We gazed upon
each other with blank faces.

'Perhaps,' said my father, ''tis additional
supply, that the General himself is taking to
the troops engaged.'   For Lundy himself
clattered by with a small escort at the moment;
they rid fast.   My father's voice was husky,
and trembled a little.

'Adam's troop had three rounds apiece served
out to them,' said Rosa.   'I know, because
Wamphray had charge of it, to take to him at
Culmore.'

'He rides,' said my father, following Lundy
with his eyes, 'like a man in earnest.'

'Will he be in earnest to make up for lost
time, do you think?' said Rosa; I had never
heard such an accent of bitterness from her
lips before.

'I doubt it,' said I; and then wished I

had said nothing to bleach her white face whiter.

At that very minute, that fear might not utterly dishearten us, came a messenger to my father, bringing news of two English ships that were in the Lough, near to the mouth of the Foyle River, bringing strong reinforcements to us. An officer, he said, had come post-haste to offer them to Lundy, but hearing where he was gone to, and that he was just too late to find him, he had turned about and gone straight back to his commander with the account of it.

The day wore on, ever the later the wearier. We never stirred abroad, Rosa and I. We strove, indeed, to employ ourselves at our ordinary tasks; but ever and anon we found our hands fallen idle before us, and ourselves into a fit of anxious musing. The least sound in the street took us to the windows; but there was nothing to be seen or heard all morning that was of the slightest interest. About two of the clock there came another message to my father, desiring his immediate presence in the council-chamber, to receive a second messenger from the ships to the Governor. So far as actual business was concerned, he might as well have stayed at home. The few persons of importance left in Derry had been duly summoned and were duly met; but Lundy had not empowered any

of them to fill his place in his absence, and consequently none of them was entitled to do so
much as make an authoritative suggestion upon
a matter referred to his decision.

So, at least, said the messenger, Major
Tiffany, who walked home from the council-
chamber with my father, there to rest and
refresh himself while he waited Lundy's return
to the city.   A bluff, soldier-like man, we
thought him, with manners that smacked more
of the camp than of the castle.   He would
speak of nothing save the defence of the city,
which, indeed, was the one subject we cared
to hear of.   But his views thereon were something disheartening.

'Your city, sir,' said he to my father, without
disguise or softening, 'is about the poorest-
placed that ever I saw to stand a siege, if it
should come to that.'

'Why so, sir?' asked my father.   'We stand
upon a fair eminence, and, sure, we have as
good a moat in front of us as heart can wish.'

'The river, you would say,' said the Major.
'Why, so it is indeed—an excellent moat, if
that were all that's needed.   But see how ill
you lie to the hills around you; they command
you on every side.   To artillery well posted
you lie as open as though you had no wall.
Why, with a good field-battery and good

gunners, I'll undertake to shell you out of your
city in three days ;—or bury you in its ruins—
which you please.'

'And yet Derry stood a good siege in '42,'
said my father, ' and, what is more, came out of
it victorious.'

'The enemy can't have understood their
advantages, that's all,' responded Major Tiffany.
' There are some among King James's generals
that do ; I can tell you that. I don't profess to
be versed in ancient history, but, if my memory
serves me at all, there were no soldiers against
you in the '42 ; nothing but wild Irishmen, with
scarce any guns, and no better instruction in
warfare.'

'I'd like to hear you tell that to the O'Neills,'
said my father, a little grimly. ' But if our
arms be successful to-day, there may be no siege
to stand.'

''Twill be ours to prevent it,' said the other
gallantly. ' But I suppose you are aware that
they're taking up their position on the other
side of the river, for all that ?'

Soon after that their conversation flagged,
and they went out together. Master Hewson
made his appearance as they left. We had
seen but little of him all day, and now he took
his customary seat without saying a word. I
know not what wrought upon the man, but he

was less sour and stern this day than ever
I saw him before ; methought, indeed, that I
discerned a gleam of human pity in his eyes
when they met mine or rested upon Rosa.

The evening began to draw down apace, and,
truly, the afternoon had passed at a rate very
different from the leaden morning. It could
not but lighten our spirits to know of friends so
near ; in force to follow up our victory, if victory
were ours ; to help us to turn the tide, if 'twere
otherwise. The same feeling was general in
the town. The assurance of their Majesties'
care for us was enough in itself to give confidence to the most timorous.

Towards dusk there fell gradually on the city
a strange, expectant hush, the pause before the
thunder-clap, it proved ; or should I liken it to
the shuddering chill that precedes the snow?
For it was broken by no ringing shout of
triumph, but by a weary lagging through the
streets of listless, dishevelled men in straggling
parties. No need to ask them how the day had
gone ; 'twas writ large upon their faces in a
character none could fail to read. These were
men in flight, and he that led them therein was
their General, Lundy.

The streets were beginning to be full of those
that had gone to meet our returning soldiers, as
Lundy rid up to his own door. Never a word

said they, bad or good, while the beaten men were passing through; but as Lundy came by there rose and grew a kind of inarticulate murmur of rage—a terrible sound, and one that even he could not disregard. He turned him on his horse to face the crowd, as though he would have addressed them. But there broke out a sudden storm of shouts and cries of execration, mixed with a hissing sound that was the very speech of indignation. Lundy was altogether daunted by it, and got himself into the safety of his house as speedily as he could.

But mine own attention was drawn away from the people in the street by the sound of weeping at my side.

'Courage, sweetheart,' said I to Rosa, as confidently as I could. 'This is but a small part of those that rid out to the muster; the rest may have had better fortune.'

'No, young mistress, nor will,' said Mr. Hewson's harsh voice from the other window—'nor will, until the armies of the Lord be purged of them that are none of His men. I marvel at nothing that comes from you,' he continued, stepping back from the window; 'but it doth strike me with wonder—ay, and with grief—to hear a man like your father speak as one that puts his trust in chariots and in horses. I marked him in the street with yonder ungodly soldier. I listened to their talk, though they were not aware of me. Verily, any man might think that it was from the English ships and soldiers he looked for salvation. He will see how far they will avail. In the streets I hold my peace, for there to speak out would profit nothing ; but among mine own flock I say fearlessly——'

'Oh, for pity's sake, Master Hewson, spare *us* your prophecies as well !' I broke in, seeing how terribly Rosa was moved by his words, and, truth to tell, not a little disappointed myself to hear him break forth in this vein ; for, from his countenance, I had judged him a little touched with feeling of our anxiety. 'For the sake of common humanity—I say not of common modesty—pretend not to lay bare the secret counsels of the Almighty, that, sure, are as little known to you as to us ;—but go out and fetch us news.'

Mr. Hewson is like a very woman, as the scurril proverb makes us, and must ever have the last word ; but this time I let him have it with all my heart, nor even heard what it was he said. For even as I begged him to go in quest of news, I saw Mr. Murray and Major Tiffany enter the house, and knew they brought it.

The Major fell at once into a vein of condoling with us and consoling us, that was little more grateful to our ears than his former conversation upon the unfitness of the city to sustain a siege; being coloured, as that was, by a persuasion of our inferiority to Richard Hamilton's troops, or, as I should say, King James's. For by this time it was known that King James, if he was not in person with his army, was following hard upon their heels.

'We bring you bad news, I'm grieved to say,' said he to us, 'the worst, in fact, though, after all, nothing more than was looked for on board when I set out. For what can you expect when raw men, that scarce have heard a gun fired in their lives, oppose themselves to regular troops? Had your Governor but advised himself to wait until we joined him, now!'

'The enemy would have been across the Fords of Fin, all the same,' said my father dryly.

'Truly! but without defeating you,' said the Major, lifting his brows, as much as to say, 'Here's an example! one that hath not the sense of warfare in him!' 'Your numbers and your courage,' he continued, 'had still been whole to give you heart to confront them nearer home. There must be advantageous ground between this and Lifford, where you could have offered battle with a prospect of success; as it is, your men will require the shelter of walls before you can bring them to face the King's troops again.'

'The King's troops'—that was what he said; but I know not whether any marked the word, save I.

'Sir,' said Mr. Murray, ' I will pardon your reflections on our courage and training, because you know nothing of either. But you shall understand that whenever our men have been brought face to face with the Irish troops they have beaten them, if our numbers have been within one to four of theirs.'

Major Tiffany gave a little mocking laugh.

''Tis strange, then,' said he; 'and you'll pardon me for pointing it out to you, that you are pushed back out of all your advanced posts, even to the last of them; till now you have little more than the ground within your walls, and must needs abide a siege here, for all I can see, or else capitulate.'

Mr. Murray flushed a deep red, and laid his hand upon his sword; for all he is so old and grave a man, I could see he was angered to the quick. But Mr. Hewson interposed with one of his long-winded orations, giving the Major to understand that his reasons for our misfortunes were all beside the mark, and ascribing that, himself, to the providence of God, which ought to have been laid at the door of the improvidence of man. He ended by describing our profanation—so he termed it—of the Sabbath, 'which in this house at least,' said he, 'was wholly without excuse, they having had the ways of godliness expounded to them from their youth up. How can they expect but that God will revenge upon them their contempt of His holy ordinances?'

The Major stared at him in astonishment.

'Sir,' said he, 'I can scarce see you for the dusk; but it's easy enough to tell your cloth in the dark, and that agrees but poorly with soldiership. If the half of what I heard rumoured in the street be true, sir, then perhaps, if instead of stopping their preparations when they did, they had carried them on all Sunday, God might have *owned them*, as you put it, with success. I must make the best of my way to the Governor, who will by this time, no doubt, be ready to receive me. But give me leave to tell you, sir, at parting, that, to the best of my poor observation, God's providence is generally on their side that show most prudence!'

With that, Major Tiffany took his leave. My father stood still in his place for many minutes, plunged in thought. Had he been the one to answer Mr. Hewson's denunciation, I little doubt but his own good sense had led him to much the same conclusion as the Major's.   But that conclusion had been put too strongly and sharply to commend itself to a mind so devout, and withal so ascetic ;—it had been so put, besides, by one that had the moment before offended him deeply.   He pondered it for awhile, and then he turned to Mr. Hewson, and spoke—spoke slowly and deliberately, after his manner when his mind is thoroughly made up.

'Master Hewson,' said he, 'I spoke to you hastily and thoughtlessly o' Saturday night; I crave your pardon for it.   The event hath proved that you were right and I—wrong.' ('Twas a frank avowal, but the word came with a hesitation and a gulp.)   'I was moved,' he continued, 'by worldly prudence ; and worldly prudence in such matters is no better than folly.   Henceforth, whatever may appear to be the necessity, neither I nor mine shall lift hand on the Lord's Day, to do aught that breaks upon its ordained rest.'

Mr. Hewson cast up his eyes with a gesture of thanksgiving.

'Did I not say,' said he, 'that the Lord would purge our defenders of all that was not to His mind?   The process is begun, and it may well be that He will save us with a poor three hundred and no more, as in Gideon's days.'

I fell into a fit of musing that closed mine ears to the rest they said. I would fain have held my peace, but it was borne in upon me that if I did so I was bound to render obedience to my father's will in this matter. And what were that, said an inner voice in mine inner ears, but to be entangled again in the yoke of bondage that I had cast aside?

After the exercise, therefore, I opened my mind to Mr. Murray, and entreated him, with all the reverence I could show him, to hold me free from the vow he had made. He looked upon me thoughtfully for a moment; then, to my thankfulness, he allowed my request.

'I pretend to no authority over you now, Mary,' said he very deliberately. 'But remember this: I made that promise for all my family. You shall do as your conscience requires of you, should difference arise; but if you go contrary to my will, you can no longer remain in my house.'

He spoke without anger, and I bowed my head in assent to what he said. When Rosa and I were left together, I found to my surprise that I was trembling.

'How could you speak so, Mary?' said she. "I cannot think how you could venture to

oppose your father and Mr. Hewson as you
did. And, forgive me, but I see you fear them
as well as I.'

'Fear Master Hewson! not a whit,' said I.
'But I did fear—and grieve—to grieve my
father.'

'Yet you did it,' said she gravely.

'I could not help it,' I replied. 'It seemed
as if, unless I said what I did, I set my hand to
a bond that might cost—I know not what;
perhaps the dearest thing I own.'

'Then, I suppose, that is what I have done,'
said she thoughtfully, after a minute's silence.
'No, I know what you would say,' she
answered to my look—I was, indeed, about
to urge her to do as I had done, and claim
her freedom—'but it's of no use. It seems to
me more my duty to be guided by men so wise
and good than to think for myself.'

To that I had nothing to answer, and therefore held my peace. She misinterpreted my
silence.

'If you think you were mistaken,' said she,
'sure, nothing can be easier than to take back
your words.'

'Nothing easier, indeed,' said I, wondering
a little to find myself smiling. 'I am even
attracted by the prospect of pleasing them
both so much, Rosa, little as I believe you

think it of me. But I fear I do not think I was mistaken.'

She gave a quick sigh.

'I wish you did,' said she, 'for that's a terrible man, Mary, and I hate to hear you brave him. See how strangely his words are always justified.'

'What, always?' said I; and I smiled again.

'Why, yes,' said she; 'I think so. He foretold us disaster on Saturday night, and it's in the very air. You yourself, now—he foretold you, that night we were so overjoyed at the news of James's return——'

She stopped there, unwilling to wound me. But she had dealt me a shrewder thrust than she knew, and one I scarce knew how to answer; for none but myself knew how deep and sore that disappointment had pierced.

It was true, besides, that once or twice a kind of loathing awe of the man's insight had oppressed me. Strange, that at my sister's words, which recalled the most extraordinary semblance of it, that shadow should pass clear off my mind, never again to vex me.

'*Overjoyed!*' I said, repeating the word she had used. 'Were we really *over*joyed, Rosa? Consider, and tell me what you think. I'd as lief take your opinion of that matter as his.'

She was silent; unable, I was assured, to approve entirely either his view or mine.

'I never can believe,' said I—and with my lips upon her brow I tried to express my pity— ay, and reverence—for the thought I could not share—'I never can believe that it is out of revenge, or out of vanity, that our heavenly Father smites us. Why, I could scarce think so meanly of Mr. Hewson himself. It is not as we punish our children, but as we teach them, that God sends pain. Believe it.'

There was a little silence.

'What then?' said she, breaking it.

'Why,' said I very gravely—for, indeed, there was a kind of weight of foresight on my own heart as I spoke—'we might shrink from the rod in the hand of anger, dearest Rosa, and small blame to us, that I can see. But, sure, we never could desire to escape from our lessons.'

And if hereby I set my hand to a bond not far different from my father's, made an hour before, 'tis one that I hope I should not shrink to make over again; for a lesson learnt is worth some pains in the conning.

CHAPTER XXVI.

TELLS HOW NEAR OUR BETRAYER CAME TO
WORKING HIS WILL.

WOULD any creature that hath ever had friends
engaged in battle believe that anything could
happen to draw away the mind from the remembrance of their danger? It seems scarce
possible, yet it is the fact that, on the morning
after Claudy Ford, it was not so much the
thought of our friends and their defeat that
filled our heads, as that of the arrival of the
English ships in the very nick of time, and
the hopes they gave us of retrieving that
defeat.

We were up betimes, and the day was
still early when we went out—truants from
home for once. For, indeed, it was more
than we could endure, to sit, as it were, just
within the sound of the news a-making, and
yet too far away to discern what it was; to be
near enough to the city's heart to share its

fever, and yet not near enough to know what set it a-beating. The heart of Derry was the Diamond. We, being just round the corner in Butchers' Street, and on the way to one of the gates, could see much of what passed; but, faith, on such a day as this 'much' was not enough for us; we desired to see all. Accordingly, as I said, we were out betimes, and took our way towards Captain Ash's house in the Diamond itself; there we were always sure of a welcome from the Captain himself and from Mrs. Browning, his kinswoman, who by this time was settled there with her little granddaughter, Mary Rankin.

We were not long in finding out that it is one thing to take one's way to a place in the heart of a city that is in a fever of warlike feeling, and quite another thing to arrive thereat. No sooner were we come into the Diamond, scarce more than a dozen steps from our own door, than we found ourselves at a standstill. All the folk in Derry, it appeared, were come together there, so that there was scarce standing-room left for us. Unless we were willing to push and jostle like any linkboy or porter, there seemed small chance that we could make our way to Captain Ash's house, near as it was.

We were wondering if there was nothing else to be done than to turn back and go home

again, when a man in front of us, hearing ou
voices, I must suppose, turned round and asked
us how we did. This was Colonel Chichester,
and he was going on to ask us what brought us
abroad on such a morning, when there came a
sound from behind us of one making his way
through the crowd in a very masterful manner.
It was Frank Hamilton, of Hamilton's Ban, and
it was clear that whosoever stood in his way
must even get out of it, and that at the best of
his speed. 'Room there, good people—room,
if you please,' was his cry. And room, sure
enough, they made. Seeing us, he stopped and
spoke ; but his greetings to Rosa and me were
of the curtest, and after them he turned to
Colonel Chichester without a moment's pause,
and 'Chichester,' says he, 'why are you not at
the council of war that is a-holding ?'

'Because I haven't been summoned,' replied
the other shortly.

'Summoned !' said Frank sharply. 'Are you
one that will wait to be *summoned*, at a moment
like this, to a council that Lundy's the president
of ? If you do, you are like to be left to wait
as long as you will.'

'Would you have me force myself upon
them ?' asked Colonel Chichester, speaking as
sharply as Frank had done.

'Name of God, sir, certainly !' he replied, his

face scarlet on the sudden. ' It's our right to be present with the rest. I know not why we should wait outside till they call us in. Do you know that there's scarce a man called to it but Lundy himself and the English officers? After yesterday, too, I wonder he hath the face !'

' Don't speak of yesterday, I beg of you,' exclaimed Colonel Chichester, reddening in his turn. ' It makes the heart burn in my breast to think of it. If that haven't humbled him, sure there's nothing will.'

' Come, then—come at once,' says Frank, ' before he have time to stuff the heads of the Englishmen with his cowardly treason.'

' But, patience, my dear man !' said the other. ' I don't like to thrust myself down the man's throat, for all that hath come and gone.'

' Don't you, indeed !' said Frank savagely, quite forgetful, I believe, of our presence. ' Then stay—stay, and be damned to you ! I would I could stuff you down his lying throat, and choke the pair of you !'

With that he turned his back upon us all, and was gone, making his way through the crowd as he had done when we first saw him. Colonel Chichester, unable, I suppose, to brook the insult of his last words, followed him. Rosa and I were left alone. We looked at each other, and then burst into a laugh ; and

having begun, we laughed as merrily as ever
we did in our lives, and it was strange to find
how much our spirits were lightened by that
laughter.

It seemed scarce possible to cross the
Diamond; we turned, therefore, and went
home; but on the threshold we met Margery,
about to go in quest of us. She had a man
with her, a servant of Sir Arthur Rawdon's;
who had come, she told us, with a message from
his master to Mr. Murray, begging him to go
to him with the news of what was doing in the
town, he being unable to stir from the house.
But my father, being called away urgently, had
sent Margery to desire we would go to Sir
Arthur in his stead, promising to visit him himself later in the day, when the decision arrived
at by the council of war should be known.

We found Sir Arthur laid upon a couch; he
was fully dressed, even to his sword; but looking so ghastly ill that we ceased to marvel that
he should be absent from his place in the
council-chamber. He endeavoured to rise to
receive us, though it was plain to any eye,
however unused to the signs of sickness, that
he was wholly unfit to sustain himself upright.
It was no easy task to bring him to admit as
much, and resign himself to continue in the
attitude in which we found him.

'You do me far too much grace,' he told us, 'to be my intelligencers, I lying here like a log the while; when all the men of the province, both old and young, are full of duty and business—as men should be.'

'Come, now,' said I, 'no moping. Haven't you been busy enough for the last three or four months to have earned a rest, even if you were not forced to take it? There's not a man in Derry to-day that hath done half as much, or will make up the difference in the next month; so take your inaction with as good grace as you can, and let others take a share of the work—'tis their turn.'

'It's sick for news you are, I believe,' said Rosa. 'I wish we had more to tell you—and better.'

'I think my complaint's the exact opposite,' said he, 'and that it's sick of news I am. If you had it better, as you say, no doubt that might make a difference.'

His words made some pretence of lightness, but his voice and his eyes, despondent as the sound of rain upon mown grass, betrayed how mere a pretence it was.

'But we have,' said I. 'There's good news this morning—the best, indeed, short of victory actually won. With the reinforcements that have arrived from England, we shall soon retrieve our failures, don't doubt it. The darkest hour, you know, is at the turn of the night.'

'That's well said,' he replied sadly. 'And they come in good time, too ; but what reinforcements, what victory, can give back wasted lives ?   I didn't altogether mean yesterday's defeat, Mrs. Hamilton, though that was heavy news enough.   I have some this morning that touches me nearer the heart, I think.   See that.'   He handed me a paper twisted and crumpled to a rag.   'Edmonston's dead,' he continued, not waiting for me to open it—'dead at Culmore ; dead !—a man you might have trusted your soul with.   And it's not starvation and exposure that have killed him, either, so much as grief and despair at the way things are going with us.'

'Don't call his life wasted!' said I.   '"Tis part of the price of the liberty of his country.'

'And God knows,' said he passionately, 'that so the purchase is effected, I grudge the life of a comrade as little as I would my own—ay, even a comrade's like Edmonston ; never man had a better.   I grudge my health as little,' says he, after a pause, 'though it's shattered, Aicken says, at eight-and-twenty ; as to mine estate, I'd never name it, used in the public service.   But if half's true that they tell me——

There came a knock at the door; and being bid to enter, Colonel Chichester walked in.

'All's up, Rawdon, I fear,' said he, after the shortest of greetings; 'the sooner we're out of this poor ill-fated place the better.'

'What do you mean? what——' said Sir Arthur, unable to find words for his question, or perhaps, in his utter weakness, unable to bring out those he had on his tongue.

'I can't tell you,' said Colonel Chichester; 'save this, that Lundy's evidently determined that none of us shall enter the council-chamber till he and the English officers have finished their discussions. That speaks for itself. There were a dozen of us, or more, in the lobby, all insisting on our right of entry; but could we get in? not though we had paved the floor with gold pieces. The sentinel told us his orders were *strict*, and that the council was desired to be kept *select.*'

Sir Arthur gave a curious quavering laugh, but still he said not a word.

'Select!' Colonel Chichester continued—'that was his word; heard you ever such an insult! As if men like the Hamiltons, Ponsonby, and Crofton weren't good enough company for the best that ever came out of England. I say nothing of myself, but it's news to me that where Lundy goes I'm not fit to come after him.'

'But, God's patience, man! surely you weren't *turned?*' broke out Sir Arthur.

'The sentinel was armed,' said Colonel Chichester, 'and we were not minded to provoke a fray.'

'Armed!' said Sir Arthur Rawdon, repeating that strange laughter that left his eyes like coals of fire, and his face like the face of a corpse. 'Armed! I tell you, Chichester, that if I could stand upon my feet, there's no sentry on his that would keep me out of a council where I had the right to be; no, nor any dozen sentries, —not while I had a sword by my side.'

'Why do you say that the city's doomed,' asked Rosa, 'because the council is kept private? For the Governor I say nothing; but the English officers, sure, are men of honour.'

'I don't know, Mrs. Murray,' said Colonel Chichester moodily. 'There's treachery in the air—of that I'm certain. For one thing, the sentry said I had been summoned in the morning, before the session of the council began; that was a lie on the face of it, because I never stirred from home till later than that, expecting that very message, which never came. If anyone was sent with it, I doubt he had his orders to seek me where I was least likely to be found.'

'How did you answer him?' asked Rosa.

'"Why, if that's the case," said I,' replied the Colonel, '"I'm here now—let me in!" "Nay," says he, "but I must first know what the Governor's mind is now;" and with that goes in and leaves us all in the lobby, like so many lackeys. When he came out 'twas with "Nay" on his lips. "The Governor," he said, "could not have the meeting interrupted, now that the business was so far advanced!" Were you sent for, Rawdon, may I ask?' says he, turning suddenly to Sir Arthur.

'If I had been,' said Sir Arthur, 'it's there I'd be this minute, and not here!'

'You couldn't have walked down,' said the Colonel, 'if you had been summoned a dozen times over.'

'That's even but too certain,' said Sir Arthur; 'but I'd not have thought a bit of shame to be carried there in a litter; no, nor to give them mine opinion lying on my back, as I am this moment. Why do you ask if I was summoned?' he ended.

'Merely because it was given out that you were,' replied Colonel Chichester, with a smile that was of the grimmest. 'I heard them saying in the lobby, as we waited—I must suppose upon Lundy's authority—that he sent for you before the sitting began, and had for answer that you were busy dying, and couldn't be troubled with affairs.'

Sir Arthur's face flushed suddenly from deadly pale to red; he blew upon his call, without replying by a word to Colonel Chichester. His servant came immediately.

'Here, you—you, Dawson,' said his master sitting up suddenly upon his couch : 'was I sent for this morning to the council? and did you return for answer that I lay dying, and couldn't be troubled with affairs?'

'Never, sir! neither came such a message, nor dared I have sent such an answer,' said the man, 'without a word to you——'

But Sir Arthur, turning round to Colonel Chichester, as though he would have spoken, fell back upon his couch in a swoon that at first we took for death. And here I had occasion to admire the behaviour of Margery, who came forward out of the window where she was in waiting for us, and, tending upon Sir Arthur with promptness and skill, presently recovered him. My father entered before he had spoken, coming in compliance with the message that he had sent him—to bring the latest news. His countenance had a more satisfied look than I had seen on it for days, but it clouded as he saw Sir Arthur's state.

'What's this?' said he, looking towards Rosa

and me with severity.   'What have you said to
him to put him in such a taking?'

'It's none of the ladies' fault, sir, but mine,'
said Colonel Chichester, with contrition.   'Telling him—things I had better have kept to
myself.   I'd never have named them if I'd
thought he'd have taken them so to heart.
Lie still, Rawdon,' he continued authoritatively,
as Sir Arthur made a motion of raising himself
on his couch again—'lie still, I say.   You're
as unfit as a baby to be troubled about things
you can't help—nor we, neither,' he added, in a
lower tone.

'I know not why we should talk of things we
cannot help,' said Mr. Murray, 'when we stand
in a better position than ever we have done yet,
to give a good account ourselves in the face of
the enemy.'

'Eh, sir, what's that you say?' exclaimed the
Colonel.   'I would fain hear more of that.
'Twas the very contrary things looked to me
when I was abroad this morning.'

And Sir Arthur, finding voice in spite of the
terrible exhaustion that was written on his face,
begged to hear what had been fixed in the
council of war.

'I was not at the council, Sir Arthur,' said
Mr. Murray, 'nor any man I know, save
Chidley Coote and Blayney.'

' But these two are worth a score,' murmured
Sir Arthur to himself.

' But I met Lundy himself in the street as
I was making my way hither,' continued my
father. ' The streets are packed—you could
scarce believe it, so empty as the town was
yesterday—and we were brought to a stand
close to each other, so that I had some little
talk with him. He told me that the English
officers were gone down to the ships to bring
up their men, and that he himself was upon his
way to Horace Kennedy upon the business of
finding them quarters. And that,' said he,
looking upon Rosa and me with a perplexed
face, ' brings me in mind of what I was considering as I was coming to this house ; which was,
how I am to get you home again. I scarce
believe that you could make your way through
the crowd even now. But you must try it, and
that without delay, for when the English troops
come into town 'twill be a manifest impossibility.'

We needed no second telling, feeling sure
that 'twas time Sir Arthur were left to himself,
but or ever we could take our leave he had
another pair of visitors. There was that in
their faces that stopped us till we should hear
their news. They were Captain Hugh McGill
and Mr. Mogredge, the Town Clerk. The latter

was evidently a stranger to Sir Arthur, for Captain McGill lost no time in presenting them to each other.

'Sir Arthur Rawdon,' said Mr. Mogredge, making his leg, 'I have not had the honour to be of your acquaintance hitherto, often as we have been in company together. But you are as little a stranger to me as you must be to any man that hath his country's prosperity at heart.'

'You flatter me, sir,' said Sir Arthur.

'I do not, indeed, sir,' replied Mr. Mogredge. 'And it's precisely the interest I take in your welfare that brings me into your house at this moment, when you are so very unfit to receive a stranger.'

'That which is a pleasure to a man rarely harms him, sir,' said Sir Arthur very civilly, 'and the company of my friends is a cordial to me.'

'Perhaps you're not aware, sir,' said Mr. Mogredge, 'that you are the only man in Derry—there are but three altogether—that is excepted by name from Tyrconnel's proclamation of pardon.'

'I desire you shall understand, sir,' replied the other, 'that I value Tyrconnel's pardon at the same rate as his threats, and that's at naked nothing. He's perfectly welcome to hang, draw, and quarter me if he likes—*on paper*. We are done with him and his master here in Derry, sir.'

'Perhaps not for ever, Sir Arthur Rawdon,' said Mr. Mogredge very gravely, whereat the face of the other flushed again that vivid colour that it had done before his swoon.

'I protest I can't understand you, sir,' said he, after a moment's pause. 'You profess to be a lover of your country, but by your words——'

He broke off without completing his sentence.

'I am indeed a lover of my country and of her friends,' said Mr. Mogredge meaningly; 'and 'tis to save one of the best of them that I entreat you to take advantage of the presence of the English ships in the river and go aboard of them. I can scarce blame you, sir, if you suspect my motives; you know so little of me. But Captain McGill will bear me witness that I mean you nothing but good.'

'That I will indeed,' said Captain McGill heartily.

Sir Arthur looked keenly at them both.

'Be more plain, sir, I beg of you,' said he, addressing Mr. Mogredge.

'I dare not, indeed, sir,' said he. 'But I speak from assured knowledge, believe me, when I say that this town may shortly be no place for any man that hath made himself so obnoxious to King James's Government as you have done.'

At this my father struck into the conversation, speaking with that deliberate openness that lends his words such weight.

'Your words would seem to point at treachery in council, Mr. Mogredge,' said he.

'Don't urge me, sir, I beg,' said he. 'I have said already that I dare not be more plain. I was present at the council in the mere capacity of clerk, as you know, and I can't betray their decision against their will.'

'I am as much at a loss as Sir Arthur,' said Mr. Murray; 'for I have parted from the Governor within the hour, and he told me that the English officers were gone back to the ships to bring up their men into the town. What could be less like the return of King James to power than that?'

'Sir,' said Mr. Mogredge, very much moved, 'are you sure that the Governor made use of these words you've repeated?'

'Perhaps not of these very words,' said Mr. Murray, 'but that was certainly his meaning.'

'Then may God forgive him!' said Mr. Mogredge passionately. 'Since he hath told you so much, I will make bold to tell you something more, even though I violate the rules of mine office by so doing. He hath told the English officers that there is not provision in the town for ten days for the number that will be in it.'

'But it's impossible, sir,' exclaimed Sir Arthur. 'It's not many weeks since I heard him say myself that the town was victualled for a year. It's not many days since he stated that the storehouses were filled to the doors; no room for the stuff that was wasting by the roadsides throughout the country!'

'Nevertheless, he hath stated at to-day's council what I tell you,' said Mr. Mogredge, 'and, what is more, his word hath passed for it with the Englishmen. Added to that, they have agreed that the town's not capable of being held, lying so exposed as it doth against an enemy well provided with artillery. So you will see, Sir Arthur, you being situated as you are, that I give you a friend's advice when I counsel you to go aboard the ships while there is time.'

'You hint at a composition, sir,' said Sir Arthur, as pale as he had been red a minute before.

'I dare hint at nothing, sir,' said Mr. Mogredge.

'Oh, but he doth,' broke in Captain McGill; 'he dare not go so far as to speak it plainly out, but what else does every word he hath said point to ?   A composition !   And how it's like to be kept by the Catholics, you know well, Sir Arthur Rawdon—you, who saw the ruffian Raps s'ab my dear and gallant young brother again and again with their bayonets, after he had yielded himself at their promise of quarter. Just such faith they'll keep with the rest of us. We know them of old.   It is truly and indeed the advice of a friend that Mr. Mogredge gives you when he says, " Begone out of reach of their malice while you have time and the opportunity." '

Sir Arthur lay back on his pillow ; he said not a word in reply.   I looked alternately at him where he lay, and out upon the growing crowd in the streets ; for, like Margery, I had withdrawn me into a window.

' If I could lift my sword !' said Sir Arthur presently, ' there is not that virtue in the tongue of man that could induce me to fly while there's the least chance—or hope.   Chichester, what say you ?'

' Oh, I'm going,' said the Colonel dryly. ' I'd take my part with any man in defending a cause, as long as there was a grain of hope— or use.   But I fail to see the sense of throwing away one's life when there's none.'

' 'Twould be criminal,' said my father very

deliberately, 'if Sir Arthur Rawdon should throw away a life so valuable to the country as his.'

At that Sir Arthur gave a low groan.

'It hath been so, indeed,' said Mr. Murray, 'and may well be so again; and I say you are bound to preserve it.'

'Then you are going too,' said Sir Arthur, addressing him.

'I, sir? No,' said Mr. Murray. 'I am an old man; I shall tarry where I am and share the fate of my neighbours. My daughters, perhaps—there's none can blame a woman any more than a man sick to death, if she withdraw herself from danger—they shall be free to do as they list.'

'I will stay where I am,' said Rosa, who sat at his side; and with the words, she put her hand in his.

'You have faith in the cause, then?' said Sir Arthur to her.

'I have faith in God, I hope,' said Rosa, with a smile that had something of the angel in it, 'and would choose to abide that which He may send.'

Sir Arthur gave a quick, sharp sigh.

'I repent me that I so much as thought of going,' said he. 'I never thought to be shamed by women and by old men; I shall stay along with you.'

' To be a care and a source of weakness to us in the struggle that's at hand !' said I from my window. I protest I never meant to say it ; I was but thinking it, and out it came.

For an hundred thoughts had been seething through my head, as I stood and listened to their talk, and watched the rabble in the street. Thoughts of my husband's desertion—I compared it with the temper of some of the gentlemen I was in company with, and it seemed but venial—the fault of a nature over-generous and headstrong, contrasted with theirs that would quit their post to ensure their own safety, not to discharge a fancied debt of honour and friendship. I contrasted it again with the conduct of our chiefs that day in council, and it appeared even praiseworthy. I looked at the faces of the men in the street, so stern, so steadfast—ay, and so strong and noble, though they were but of the baser sort for the most part; and I was struck with both admiration and confidence. And then a foolish thought possessed me, that perhaps I was set here in his place, so that my faithfulness might atone for his error. I was persuaded that the struggle was nothing near finished, whatever the captains might do or think ; and, like my father, I determined to stay and cast in my lot with my fellow-citizens.

Sir Arthur looked up from his couch at my words. I read his thoughts in his face, and he read mine.

'You have not lost faith in the cause, at any rate,' said he.

'The contrary,' said I quickly. 'It's presumption, no doubt, to say it, in opposition to the opinion of so many of our leaders; but I never felt greater hope of it than at this moment. Shall I tell you what I see from this window? The people stand in the street as thick as bees a-hiving; their eyes burn steady fire; their mouths are shut, like steel traps for firmness; their hands are clenched, as though they would fight the enemy with their fists, rather than turn their backs on them—ay, and they'd do it, too, as blithely as ever they went to a feast. I would not for all the treasure in England be the man to go out and tell them a capitulation was agreed to. I'd stake the last penny I own, that man would never stand in the safety of his house again—he'd be torn limb from limb where he stood. Now, do you despair?'

For it was borne in upon me that it was nothing but despair that was killing him, as he said it had killed Colonel Edmonston.

'I scarce can tell you,' said he wearily. 'If they had but the leader you speak of! I would that I were the man. But wanting him, what are they? A mere rabble—chaff, to be blown away before the wind of the Irish army!'

'I fear,' said Colonel Chichester sadly, 'that's but over-true an estimate.' The others held their peace.

I crossed the room to the side of Sir Arthur's couch.

'You have been the man ere this,' said I to him; 'and you may be again, if you will but get you gone into safety, as your friends desire you. For the rest, trust in God, as my sister said. When He hath so marvellously prepared the heart of even "the rabble," as you call them, sure, He won't deny them a leader—'twere impiety to think so.'

CHAPTER XXVII.

THE LAST AND WORST OF LUNDY'S TREACHERY.

EARLY the next morning Wamphray came to the house, scarce able to take pleasure in the sight of us for chafing that he had been denied speech of the Governor, to whom he bore a message from his cousin and Colonel, Adam Murray. It was so great a joy to know him alive and well, that it drove the remembrance of our misfortunes out of our heads for a time, but not for long. He himself recalled them to our minds, partly by the lowness of his spirits, and partly by his talk, that ran constantly on the defeat at Claudy Ford.

'But there's one consolation,' said he, 'and that is, that I've seen Adam fight—'tis a great sight. Now, how little we know a man, even an ancient comrade, until we have seen him striving in his proper calling! I've been used to think myself in some sort Adam's equal. Faith, now I know better, I assure you! I would I could think myself capable of carrying out his orders as they should be executed.'

'Ah, well,' said Rosa; 'but you forget you're no more than a beginner in the calling that Adam has passed his youth at. You can't be expected to gather in a few weeks the experience that he hath gotten in the course of years and years.'

'No,' said Wamphray, 'nor ever shall, even in the course of years. And if you ask the reason, it is that Adam hath the leader's gift by nature; and I, merely the follower's—if, indeed, I have that.'

'I doubt this humility is too sudden to last,' said Rosa, smiling. 'In truth, I think it something over-strained, even as it is.'

'It's a sum in the rule of three,' said Wamphray. 'Franky Hamilton, say, is worth ten of me in the field; Adam's worth a thousand of him. What doth that come to?'

'To an exaggeration,' said I.

'Not a bit, indeed,' said Wamphray quickly. 'He is the eye to see, and the head to direct; we are but hands to execute—and that's not much. Had he had three hundred horse under him yesterday instead of thirty—well, there would have been another tale to tell, that's all.'

'What kind of tale?' asked Rosa.

'A tale of King James's horse driven back to the very sea at Dublin, I think,' said Wamphray, reddening. 'Drowned in it, perhaps. We'd have driven them before us with our swords, when powder and shot gave out.'

'Was it, then, the want of ammunition?' said I.

'Partly,' said he; 'but chiefly the utter want of any scheme of battle. We were placed altogether at random. Some say worse, that we were posted ill on purpose; and I partly believe it. For, in a random disposition, it might well have happened that some of the regiments should have been so placed as to support each other; as it was, there was nothing of the kind. Each party might fight for its own hand, Ishmael fashion; but for giving or getting assistance, it was out of the question. There was always a morass, or a hedge, or something cutting us off.'

'It must have been enough to drive you mad,' said I.

'It was,' said he, 'even to the eye of a novice. But what was that, even, compared to the order to retire, given at the very critical moment of the battle? That was enough to drive us mad indeed! Figure it! The enemy had just forded the river; they were staggering from exhaustion; they were stumbling up the bank;

a single resolute charge would have driven
them back into the water.   And just as we are
about to deliver that charge, comes the order to
retire; Lundy himself, who had but newly
arrived upon the scene, setting the example
with a very good will.'

'But, good lack!' said I, 'sure you did not
heed it ?'

'We did indeed, to our shame and sorrow,
said he.   'The very men that would have
fought like lions, had they been led, ran like
hares when they were led backwards.   'Twas
the most disgraceful affair you can picture.'

'Was it treachery indeed,' said I, 'or only
criminal folly ?'

'Treachery, past doubt,' said he.   'Any of
us that doubted that had our doubts set at rest
when, halfway to Derry, we met the waggons
of ammunition, that should have been on the
ground early in the morning, going express to
be booty to the enemy.   That disaster was
averted, by the sense of a few, much to Lundy's
grief, I'll be sworn.   Nor was that the worst.
I dare say you know that when we came to the
gates we found them shut in our faces—by
the Governor's orders, they assured us.   Had
Hamilton's army pushed on as they should, not
a man of us had been left alive o' Monday night
to tell the tale I'm telling.

'But,' says he presently, 'I'm forgetting mine errand, which is to that same Lundy, when he will be pleased to receive me.'

And so he went in search of him.

It was more than I could fathom, this of sending for orders to a man that had not only betrayed us again and again, but was known to have done so.

Whatever the reason, Lundy had yet no mind to grant him an interview. It was some hours later that he and my father, coming to the house together, were met upon the doorstep by Mr. George Walker, the late Rector of Dungannon, who had taken a house a few doors from ours. They were fallen into talk about that very matter—of Wamphray's message and the Governor's refusal to be seen—when the man himself turned into the street. He came towards them without the least hesitation; perhaps he thought valour the better part of discretion for once; or perhaps he thought he had thrown dust in their eyes so effectually that there was nothing to be feared from their penetration. Whatever his thoughts, he saluted them with perfect self-possession, and would have passed on; but Wamphray stopped him.

'I crave your pardon, sir,' said he, 'for the liberty I take in speaking first, especially in the

presence of my elders.   But if you would be
pleased to give me your answer to the paper I
left at your house this morning, I'd be deeply
grateful.   I may tell you that I've called for it
twice since then.'

'All in good time, young sir,' said Lundy
haughtily.   'I shall think the matter over in
the course of the day, and if you will call upon
me in the evening, I shall then have written
orders ready for you to take to your Colonel.'

'I must beg your indulgence, sir, if I over-
step my duty,' said Wamphray ; ' but could you
not let me have them now by word of mouth ?
You may rely upon my absolute fidelity in
repeating them.'

'I'm neither accustomed nor disposed, sir,'
said Lundy, 'to take suggestions from my
inferior officers.'

'Pardon me, my good sir,' struck in Mr.
Walker ; ' if the young man hath no title to
offer suggestions, perhaps you will listen to
one from me ; and I should say, like him, that
it's certainly time Captain Murray had his
directions.   He hath lain two nights without
the city wall to my certain knowledge, sir, for
we rid up to the gates together on Monday, to
find them shut upon us ; not a little, I may say,
sir, to our astonishment.'

Mr. Walker spoke with some heat ; his

manner betokened offended dignity, as of one that thought himself to have been treated below his consequence.

'My good sir,' replied Lundy quickly, anxious to turn their minds from the main issue, 'don't suppose that it cost me no pain to turn my brother officers from the gates—nothing, indeed, save the most imperative necessity would have forced me to it. But you are too good a soldier, sir, in spite of your cloth, not to see what a matter of paramount importance it is to husband the stores when a place hath a siege to stand, as in my poor opinion it doth appear that this ill-fated city must do it or else capitulate.'

'In mine, sir, it appears of equal importance, at least, to husband the men,' said Mr. Walker, falling straightway into the trap.

But Wamphray was more tenacious.

'All this is beside the question, gentlemen both,' said he impatiently, 'if you'll pardon me for saying so ;—which is not what ought to have been done on Monday night, but what is best to be done to-day. Am I to have the orders without which my Colonel can't act, sir, or not ?' said he to Lundy, who looked at him with a face of supercilious displeasure.

'Your young cockerel "craws crouse," Mr. Murray, as we say in Scotland,' said he, turning to my father. 'And yet I think it is but a

week or two that he commenced his military
education.'

'He knows what you, perhaps, are ignorant
of,' said my father, 'that King James's forces
are come as near to the city as to St. Johnstown,
and may, perhaps, be pardoned if he is anxious
to see proper orders given in time *for this once*,
having seen a battle lost on Monday through
nothing else than the lack of them.'

My father spoke with the air of a judge;
Colonel Lundy both winced and reddened.

'Lost through lack of proper orders, sir!'
said he, with heat. 'I protest I can't follow
you; I wonder to hear you, indeed. How
could raw men like ours face regular troops?
Was it not best to withdraw them before they
were all cut to pieces?'

'The same raw men that you speak of so
disparagingly,' said Mr. Walker, in a tone of
offence, 'have beat the Catholics a dozen times
under mine own poor leading.'

'And, sir,' my father continued, in his
severest tone, 'if the popular report be true,
you have even now sent away the trained
soldiers that by your own showing might
have opposed the Catholic army with some
hope of victory.'

'Sent them away, sir! How is that?' asked
Lundy. 'It seems that the popular report

goes further than there's book for. The ships
are still in the river; the officers have but
gone down to bring up the men.'

' Are we to take this statement as made upon
your honour, most worshipful Governor ?' said
Wamphray, contempt stinging through his words

' You push your privilege of ignorance very
far, young gentleman—very far indeed,' said
Lundy, in a voice that shook with anger.
' Were the time convenient, I would make it
some of my business to teach you better
manners.'

' Because,' continued Wamphray ruthlessly,
taking no manner of heed of his anger, ' it doth
seem that the popular rumour takes some colour
of likelihood when we hear that almost all the
men of consequence are leaving the city, and
getting them aboard of these same ships.'

' And I myself heard that account given but
last night of your intentions and actions, sir,'
said my father, ' that if they be truly what you
profess, you should lose no time in making
them public ; you may prevent much mischief
thereby.'

' For mine intentions, sir, they have ever
been as open as the day,' replied Lundy, ' let
mine enemies say what they will, and those
that let their judgment be warped by failure.
But for those leaving the town that can't fight,

I own it hath my approval ; 'tis not merely that
we are benefited by the removal of useless
mouths ; but if, as seems too likely, we be
beaten in spite of all, then many good men and
true are out of the way of danger—some of
them men excepted by name from the pro-
clamations of mercy.'

He saw that he had a little impressed Mr.
Walker and Mr. Murray by his seeming
candour, and he continued, addressing them
and quite ignoring Wamphray :

'If the time served, I doubt not but that
I could show you reason good enough, and
such as you would both approve, for all I have
done. But when I tell you that I'm on my
way at this moment to the council-chamber to
receive a messenger from that very army at
St. Johnstown whereof you did me the honour
to suppose me ignorant, you will agree with me,
I'm sure, that I have spent long enough in talk,
however valuable, for the present.'

With that, and a very courtly bow, he left
them ; but the good impression he had made
could not stand the test of five minutes' reflection, for the reasons he had given were in too
barefaced contradiction to what he had said so
often and so lately of the great plenty he had
collected of every sort of provision and munition.
Wamphray was highly indignant at his effrontery

and pressed his opinion upon the other two in a way that assuredly he had not ventured, even so short a time ago as on Sunday; so that we could not but admire how important a part of a man's education is action, and how quickly it takes effect. I could scarce believe that this man, so frank, so bold, so able to hold his own even in the presence of his elders, was my shy and submissive brother Wamphray. Mr. Murray looked at him once or twice, as though doubting the evidence of his ears, yet I saw he liked the change. Mr. Hewson, putting himself forward to rebuke it, was himself rebuked and taught to know his place for the future—a thing that mightily delighted me, though I looked down at my plate and said nothing.

As soon as dinner was over, Wamphray went out.

'I must find out one of the officers of the watch for to-night,' said he, 'and make sure of being allowed to pass in through the gates, if I return late from Culmore, as is most likely.'

'You are going to Adam without leave from the Governor, then?' said Mr. Murray.

'Certainly,' said Wamphray. 'I desire to tell him how the Governor tenders us, and what kind of orders he is like to send.'

'You know, of course, that it's an act of mutiny you're about to commit,' said my father.

'Towards Lundy, no doubt,' said Wamphray; 'but it's the last of my thoughts to show him reverence at the expense of the country's service. Sure, you would never bid me?' he asked of Mr. Murray, to which his father replied by bidding him God-speed on his errand.

As far as the fear of mutiny was concerned, 'twould have been most inconsistent on Mr. Murray's part if he had forbidden it to his son, seeing he practised it himself that very afternoon; being one of that deputation that went down to the English ships, to invite Colonel Cunningham to assume the government of the place instead of Lundy. When they came back with 'No' for their answer, there sprang up in the town a discontent that bade fair to grow into a riot. Mr. Murray was deeply grieved, especially when once or twice there were shots fired.

'But I can't blame them,' said he, 'seeing what they see—that the men of position are all leaving them, and that neither officers nor troops come back from the ships—it's but natural that they should draw their own conclusion. I can scarce blame Cunningham, either,' said he, a little later, 'for a man must be very sure he is in the right before he dare take the command out of the hands of his superior officer. But mark my words,' he continued, after a silence, 'the citizens are growing dangerous. As to the soldiers, they are dangerous already. The sending of the deputation to St. Johnstown, and the news that King James is there in person with his army, hath run like wildfire through the city, and driven them all furious. It may well prove that Lundy hath wakened up a wild beast where he meant to lull a tamed one to sleep, and I'd never marvel if it proved his destruction yet, little as he thinks it.'

But after nightfall the crowd in the streets melted gradually away, until, by bedtime, the guards had it all to themselves as usual. Bedtime came in our house the same as elsewhere, but it was allowed to pass without notice; for no thought had we of retiring until we should see our mutineer returned and safe.

He had been absent so long that we began to be a little restless, though cheering each other with the reflection that many a simple thing might happen to delay a foot-passenger. Towards eleven of the clock there came the sound of marching feet hurrying through the streets, that were by that time empty and silent, and rang to the sudden noise. Some of us thought we could distinguish Wamphray's voice as the party passed our house; but he did not enter; and we were fain to think ourselves mistaken, though with a doubt that increased our restlessness.

About half an hour later he came in, with a face as white as ashes, so that Rosa ran to him with a cry, fearing he had come by some wound. But it was not hurt of body that had so blanched his countenance.

'Sir,' said he to my father, 'all the treachery that hath been suspected is trifling compared to the thing which we have just discovered; and, thank God, thwarted.'

My father looked up at him with a face as white as his own. Wamphray drew Rosa to him, and continued:

'It's by the merest chance—or rather, I should say, by God's providence alone—that these dear eyes will open on to-morrow's light!'

His voice, as well as his aspect, gave ample confirmation of his words, so that I found myself trembling before I heard the thing I was to tremble at.

'I had been to Culmore, sir,' continued Wamphray, 'according to my intention. I had seen Adam, and was returning to the city. Acting as I was doing, without orders, it would have been my best plan to take the round-about to Butchers' Gate, where I could easily have got admittance, and from which I could have made my way to this house without risk of notice. It was what I meant to do when I left Adam; but—by God's special good care of us,

I must believe—I fell into so deep a fit of musing that I kept the Strand without consideration, and came, of course, to the Ship-quay Gate instead.'

By this time we were all got to our feet, and were hanging on his words as though we knew what was coming.

'Never a word of challenge was I met with,' continued Wamphray, 'so I laid my own hand on the handle of the gate ; found it yield to me as easily as the handle of the door of this room, and with no more noise ; and, it's the truth I'm telling you, I was among the guard—there were but four of them—before ever they knew it.'

'They had been tampered with!' said my father, drawing a long breath.

'Not a doubt of it. I should think,' said Wamphray, 'that they're half-way to St. Johnstown by this time. I never said a word to them, bad or good, but ran at the top of my speed to Crofton, who's the officer of the watch, and who turned out in less time than it takes to tell it. Bishop's Gate was found to be in exactly the same case as the other ; and there also there were but four men on guard. Crofton was told, in answer to his inquiries, that it was the Governor in person that went the rounds to-night at the time of the locking-up of the gates ;

and now the keys are nowhere to be found. What do you think of that?'

'It's only too easy to draw the conclusion,' said my father.

'Oh, and I haven't told you the whole,' continued Wamphray bitterly. 'Both gates moved so easily upon their hinges that they made hardly a sound; that struck Crofton at once, and he examined them. They turned out to be newly oiled: what was that for? That hadn't been done without the Governor's connivance, if, indeed, it weren't the work of his own hands.'

My father wiped his brow, which was beaded with moisture.

'He hath gone about to procure our destruction,' said he.

'That's neither more nor less than the truth,' said Wamphray. 'It's a miracle, nothing else, that we shall not all be massacred in our beds before morning. But we are safe, thank God, for this night; the watch is under the command of a man that can be trusted. He hath doubled the guards and changed the word; and if the enemy come, they'll meet with a reception that will astonish them. But I do not think they will come. Their accomplices have fled, as I told you; and doubtless they are aware by this time that their designs are frustrate and hopeless.'

CHAPTER XXVIII.

NO SURRENDER.

COLONEL MACDONNEL of Colkitto vaunts himself, I am told, to have a kind of supernatural insight into the future, that he says belongs only to persons of Celtic descent. I have no desire to dispute their monopoly; nor do I know, indeed, why they should pride themselves upon the possession of so discomfortable a power. But this I know, that no second-sight, no ghostly prophecy, could have increased the certainty I felt that the morrow should see either the turning-point of our fortunes, or else the commencement of our utter ruin.

Sure, it needed little insight to know as much as that. The top of the hill is the point of the watershed. The stag that is hunted to the crag-foot knows as well as his pursuers that there he must conquer or there die. In like case were we; our enemies approaching us upon three sides, and our retreat upon the

fourth all but cut off; in fact, for the great
bulk of us there was no possibility of retreat.
Should we submit our neck to the old sorry
yoke we had cast off? or should we turn at
bay, single-handed against all the rest of the
kingdom?

There seemed little choice, and so I kept
telling myself. Our leaders, beaten after incredible hardship and devotion, had left us
almost to a man—some in sore sickness, the
consequence of these very efforts that had been
brought to naught; others in utter despair of
our fortunes. The men of influence and
position, who might have taken their places,
were following them at the best of their speed—
a proceeding that was eloquent of their conviction. Were it not utter folly and presumption in a scanty remnant to endeavour afresh
what the whole strength of the province had
failed in? Were 'the rabble' to lift the
weapons which their natural chiefs had thrown
down, what could they deserve but to be annihi-
lated? Or what else could they expect?

So, over and over again, I told myself all
the morning. But ever, in spite of my wisdom,
there rose before my mind the vision of the
crowd that had filled the streets for the last two
days. I saw the set faces, fearless and stern;
the strong hands that did but wait for weapons

to wield them right grandly; and then I felt,
what I scarce dared think, that the last word of
the quarrel was not spoken when our leaders
bade us farewell.

Alas! the day was young yet, when even I
must have confessed, had any asked me, that
the time was past for any action that could be
of the smallest use.

I was out in the streets with Wamphray, and
the reason of it was this: There had come from
the Governor himself a message to Mr. Hewson,
desiring his presence at the council that was a-
holding; Wamphray also was summoned, to
receive those orders for his Captain that had
been withheld the day before. And to me
there came a message from Mrs. Browning,
telling me that one of Thomas Ash's infant
children was sick, of something that puzzled
both herself and Mrs. Gardner, his sister, and
asking me, when I could find the time and
opportunity, to go and see it. I therefore desired Wamphray to take me with him as far as
Thomas Ash's house in the Diamond, to which,
after a little persuasion, he consented.

The streets were full of people, but nothing
near so crowded as on the two previous days;
their talk, as we passed, was all of King James,
his reported presence with the army, and whether
that report could by any possibility be true; of

his envoy, who was even at that moment
closeted with the Governor and council; and
of the summons that had been sent to the Nonconformist ministers to attend, which had put
some simple souls in hope that now at last
decisive steps were about to be taken. They
made way for us to pass without the least difficulty, being as orderly and civil as one could
wish to see them; though none the readier for
that to permit themselves to be sold and deceived with tame submission.

We were arrived at Thomas Ash's door, and
were but waiting admittance, when there re-
sounded from the Double Bastion the report of
a great gun; 'twas as unexpected as lightning
from a clear sky, and as sudden in its effect.
The crowd, that a moment before had stood so
quiet, fell to running, as fast as its own numbers
would admit of, to the walls. We lost no time
in getting us within the shelter of the doorway,
which was opened to us with a question, what
the firing could signify.

'There is but one thing it can signify,' said
Wamphray, 'and that is that the enemy is come
within range.' And so got him gone towards
the council-chamber as quick as we to the
windows—Mrs. Browning and I, Mrs. Gardner,
and the three children, who clung to our skirts,
half in curiosity, half in terror. And the terror

got the upper hand when presently there came
another tremendous report from the Double
Bastion.

Hard upon that came three men in uniform
into the Diamond, attended by a drum, which
they caused to beat for silence ; and having
obtained a hearing, they made known to all
whom it might concern this notice :

'That, forasmuch as the King in person is
with his army before the gates of the city,
therefore the Governor commands and pro-
claims that the citizens and garrison maintain
quietness and order, both in the streets and on
the walls, while the negotiations are pending ;
and he who shall do aught to provoke his
Majesty's displeasure upon us, whether by
seditious shoutings, firing of guns, or in what
other manner soever, shall be held guilty of
high treason, and to have incurred the pains
and penalties attached to the same.'

If the Governor had heard the babel of
murmuring that broke out as soon as the proclamation was made, it might have given him
pause in the midst of his traitorous negotiations.
That there was treason going, sure, we were all
agreed ; only, while he ascribed it to the citizens,
they, with more reason, ascribed it to himself.
The noise of these 'seditious shoutings,' that
were forbidden, increased until they bade fair

to grow to a riot; but soon there came one
down the street that spoke to the people right
and left, and a little soothed them. This was
Mr. George Walker, on his way, he told them,
to speak to Captain Adam Murray, at the Ship-
quay Gate. After he had passed, the noise of
the murmuring died away until it was possible
to hear the words of it, which were all of
Lundy's treason: how we were sold by him
into the enemy's hands; how we had no course
open to us save to submit, being fast entangled
in the toils. 'Not a captain left us,' they said
bitterly—'not one. Had we but *one man* that
would guide us, sure, we'd follow him to death.
But there is not one—not one!' And we at the
window above them echoed the words, 'Not
one!' Truly, it seemed that the knell of our
hopes and efforts was struck, and that it was of
no use to strive against our fate any more.

Suddenly there arose a noise of shouting in
Silver Street that sent the blood through my
veins, and set my heart a-beating quicker than
the firing of the gun had done. There passed
a strange tremor through the crowd below, and
with one consent they turned their faces in the
direction of the sound. They could see no
more than we what caused it; but to them
as well as to us 'twas plain that it suggested
hope. Distant and half heard though it was,

we knew in a moment that this was no feigned rejoicing, put on to flatter a victor. There was no uncertainty about this shouting; it rang true.

It seemed as our souls must fly out of our straining eyes and ears to discover what was coming; but neither chafing nor guessing could either hasten it or inform us; there was nothing for it but to take good grasp of our patience, and wait till the newcomer should come in sight. Ever the nearer and the clearer came the shouting, and ever the clearer it grew the gladder it rang. The men in the Diamond began to take it up. I had in my hand a little wooden plaything belonging to one of the children, and presently I found that I had crushed it to atoms without knowing it, while trying to curb my passion of impatience.

Louder and louder grew the shouting, surer and surer the note of joy therein. It was indeed the mightiest anthem of thanksgiving that ever I heard in my life, though the music of it was nothing but the bursting gratitude of ten thousand hearts. 'Twas a kind of speech easy to comprehend, though inarticulate; and 'salvation' could not have been plainer spoken, though an angel had pronounced it from the sky.

A minute after the hero of it all came riding out of Ship-quay Street into the Diamond, and it was Adam Murray, none else, mounted on his great black horse, and followed by a few men of his troop.

Mr. Walker walked beside him, his hand on Adam's bridle-rein ; the old man had a spring in his gait, a fire in his eye, that seemed to have struck ten years from his age since he had passed down the street half an hour before. What spirit of prophecy seized the people I know not, but the acclamations that rang through the Diamond showed they knew that they had found their leader at last. They crowded about him, so that his great horse had no power to stir ; they touched his hands, his sword, his very bridle ; they stretched out their clasped hands towards him, as though, like an angel of God, he had power to save them by his mere word or look ; they cried to him to be their Governor, their General ; 'twas a very tumult of welcome. And yet, for all their professions of loyalty and devotion to his word, he could not at first get silence to speak to them, though he beckoned with his hand for it over and over again. But at last he obtained it, though we at the window could not hear him even then, by reason of the seething of the crowd in their efforts to be silent and to hearken.

'One of the English officers,' he was saying

when I could make out his words, ' told him to his face, I believe, that quitting of Derry was quitting of the kingdom. Look you, men, that's God's truth, and none can deny it. We have lost every place we owned, save this town alone. We've been pushed back out of Hillsborough, out of Dungannon, out of Coleraine ; we are ousted from Lifford, Strabane, Carrigans, St. Johnstown. What can we do—where can we fall back upon—if we lose Derry as well ? Ireland will belong to King James again from sea to sea, and I needn't ask you if that's what you desire.'

At that there arose such a shouting of ' No !' and ' Never !' that his voice was fairly drowned in it. But in a minute he made it heard once more.

' " Never," you say, and " Never," say I, too, with all my heart. But you know that that's what your precious Governor is busy about this very minute, drawing up a capitulation to be sent to King James, who's waiting at the end of the Windmill Hill till the gates are opened to him.'

At this again there was a storm of execration, as great as a moment before ; but his strong voice quickly mastered it.

' But who's to open them if you, the citizens, refuse your consent ? And who's to compel

you to consent against your will ? What's the
value of Lundy's composition unless you ratify
it ? And, in the name of all you care for,
what's to induce you to ratify a vile treaty
made by a knave and coward for your destruction and his own gain ?'

Faith, the walls of the council-chamber must
have been of the thickest if Lundy did not hear
in it the shout of defiance that rose at that
moment in the Diamond without.

'Listen to me, men,' said Adam, rising in his
stirrups, and looking round about upon the
crowd that packed the Diamond as far as he
could see. 'Listen, I say. You see those
gallant gentlemen behind me ? Do you know
that I had some ado to restrain them an hour
ago, when we caught sight of King James's
army, from charging into the midst of them to
try how many lives they could sell their own
for ? That was mere madness, for a small
company ; but here—why, I see an army in
front of me, and not a man of you, I believe,
but is ready to do the same thing.'

Sure enough, for another cheer, not to be
suppressed, interrupted him ; but it was speedily
silenced, and he continued :

'I knew it, for are we not all of one mind ?
and when have we ever had our will ? Checked,
and hindered, and held back at every point,

whose fault is it that we are brought to this? It's none of our own, that I'm sure of, and that we'll show them before they are many hours older. But,' says he, pulling himself up, as it were, 'it's not a battle we must fight—that would be a pleasure in the temper you've shown me—we have harder work before us. We are come to that pass, men, that we must either stand a siege in our city or let the Governor have his will. I needn't ask you which it is to be.'

Truly he needed not, for he had had one answer already, and presently he had another that out-matched it. All the pent-up rage and relief, despair and hope, that had filled the hearts of these men for the last three days, found vent in the ringing, deafening cheers that pealed out around him, and were taken up by the people that were out of sight in the other streets, until it verily seemed as though the whole city had gone shouting mad. Again and again Adam raised his hand for silence, but not until they had tired themselves with shouting did he obtain it.

'I am answered, and answered well,' said he, when at last he could make himself heard. 'But, men, I were unworthy of your confidence if I let you think that this was like to be a short and easy struggle—a week of fighting, and after

that victory.   This little corner is all that stands
between King James and the sovereignty of
Ireland; not a doubt but he and his generals
will do their best to crush us.   It will be a
struggle to the death.   Are you ready for that?
It may cost you suffering worse than death
before you see their backs.   Are you ready for
that?   Are you willing to defend the city to
the last drop of your blood, to the last pulse of
your hearts?   Hardship or no hardship, is there
to be *no surrender?*'

'Twas the very thing they lacked—a watch-
word; and he had taught it to them.   'No
Surrender! No Surrender!'   The words went
ringing through the Diamond, and far beyond
it, like the answering cheer he had provoked,
till the enemy on the Windmill Hill must have
heard them as well as we.

'Then,' says Adam, 'there remains but one
thing to be done: we must know our friends;
and to that end we must have a badge.   What
shall it be?   I know,' said he, pulling out his
handkerchief and binding it about his arm; 'let
it be this.   Let every man that is—I say not
willing, but *determined*—to follow me, tie a
band of white about his left arm, as I have
done.   'Twas the badge of the Catholics long
ago, when they were ready to murder every
Protestant—as they are now.   Let us change

its meaning, and make it the badge of Protestants that are ready to die for their faith and
country.'

He had scarce finished speaking ere there
was such a tearing of kerchiefs around him as
sure was never seen before since Derry was a
city. And presently every man in the street
was decorated like himself. The men that were,
as he said, determined to support him in the
course of ' No surrender,' were, to speak by the
book, simply every man in Derry that was
worth his salt.

Mr. Walker, decorated like the rest, was seen
to speak to him ; the people stood silent to
hearken.

' Are you going to tell all this to the
Governor ?' was what he asked.

' Straight,' said Adam. And methought his
look was something grim.

CHAPTER XXIX.

A HAPPY REVOLUTION.

LUNDY, in his president's chair, at the head of the council-board, surrounded by near all the men of consequence and repute that his practices had left in the city; the treaty of surrender upon the table in front of them, drawn up fair and full, lacking but the signatures, and these for the most part promised—did he not seem too near the point of success to be baulked? Adam Murray at the Ship-quay Gate, with a dozen men to his back—was he not to all appearance an adversary scarce worth taking note of—too contemptibly weak to be feared? And King James, with his army of five-and-twenty thousand men, advanced as near to us as to the Upper Strand—were they not a power great enough to enter those gates that Lundy was so desirous to set open to them; to possess the city, whether that *cowardly rabble* left in it consented or no; and with the city, to enter upon possession of the whole of Ireland?

Faith, it seemed so to us, left in Captain Ash's house to wait for tidings, and Mrs Gardner maintained it even with tears. With such a power as the Catholic army at his back, could not Lundy afford to laugh at Adam, even though the streets were lined with those that had sprung to range themselves behind him? It seemed no equal match. Their opposition might be, as the saying hath it, 'a nut to crack'; but with such a pair of levers as James's army and the treaty of capitulation in the hands of our commissioned Governor, it seemed an easy thing to crush it and be done with it.

And yet, scarce a couple of hours had passed before it was plain, beyond question, that Lundy's power was the thing that had been crushed. The change that passed over the demeanour of the waiting crowds showed that as clear as dawn in the sky shows that night is done. Much the same kind of change, too; from darkness to light; from impotent, angry despair, to hope and action. A stir and a shaking began everywhere at once, like that the prophet saw among the dry bones. As in that vision bone came together to his bone, and flesh clothed them, so with us: the separate members found each his fellow, joined themselves into a body forthwith, and became a living power. The men that had stood idle in the streets—together, yet single; even what they were deridingly called, a mere rabble—found themselves of a sudden transformed into orderly regiments fit for service, officered by men of their own choosing; who, they knew, would lead them with both discretion and valour.

Never was there a revolution more thorough nor more beneficent; and as for Lundy's authority, Haman's of old was not cast down more completely nor more irretrievably. But of the manner of it we could gather little at the time. They that conduct such movements, even upon so small a scale as in the government of a single city, have their hands too full to find time to answer questions.

But we, though trustworthy accounts of all that had passed would have been welcomer to us than rain to parched meadows, were so satisfied with the new aspect of things that we could make a shift to possess our souls in patience, until such time as our friends should be able to give them to us.

Next day there was the same press and bustle of business, and again 'twas only the barest outline thereof that came to our ears. That a new council had been called, and was sitting for the purpose of choosing a Governor in Lundy's stead, was noised throughout the town; and we were astonished to hear it presently rumoured that Major Baker and Mr. George Walker were pitched upon to fill the office conjointly, for we had no thought but that it should have been Adam. But he, the rumour went, was named Colonel of the Horse, and General in the field, which was, we knew, an appointment more to his mind. News, that day, spread like wildfire. That an envoy was come from King James, to discover what delayed the capitulation, was known throughout the town before the man had got him well within the doors of the council-chamber. Methinks he had little need to go there for his answer, but might well, if he were a person of any discrimination, have read it in the faces of the townsmen and in the aspect of the streets. And after that we heard that Adam was gone out of the town to settle the business of the Articles of surrender by himself alone, upon our part, with King James's representatives. It seemed as though the enemy had made very sure of us indeed, and it was hardly possible to wait patiently for the account of that interview. But what they were saying in the streets, that we said in the house—that we were in Adam Murray's hands, and therefore were safe.

Later in the day there came to be held in my father's house, in the most natural manner in the world, what I might truly describe as

another council of war, for there were present
our new-appointed Governors, both of them;
Adam Murray, who, if he was not equal to
them in dignity, was superior to them in influence; and my father and Wamphray, both
members of the new council; besides Mr.
Hewson, who cannot be kept out of any business
that is done in Mr. Murray's house. And the
business they came together to debate was,
'What's to be done with Lundy?' who kept his
chamber, very wisely, since his life (as had been
said in my hearing a dozen times over) had not
been worth a minute's purchase had he been so
ill-advised as to appear in the public streets.

Mr. Walker, we perceived, had a little gained
in consequence and dignity already, since his
new appointment. He seemed surprised and
not best pleased that Mr. Hewson set himself
down with the rest to share their deliberations.

'Sir!' said he pompously, 'I'm aware that I
ought to know your name. I regret to say it
hath escaped my memory.'

'My name, sir,' said the other, looking at him
from under his brows, every whit as sternly as
Mr. Walker's regard was haughty, 'is Hewson.'

'Ah, I remember,' said Mr. Walker; 'you
are he that came from Scotland to swear us all
to the Covenant.'

'Nay, sir,' said the other; 'I am no more

than a near relative of that good man—being, in fact, his brother.'

It was evident that Mr. Walker longed to bid him withdraw, but none of the others seemed like to back him in the request, and he forbore to make it. He went straightway and established himself in my father's great chair at the head of the table; whereat my father raised his brows, but sat down without a word next to Adam. Rosa and I would have withdrawn ourselves, knowing that 'twas our duty, though much against our will, but Adam called to us to stay where we were.

'For this,' said he, 'is no formal council, but a mere friendly discussion; and, sure, a woman's wit may see a way through many a maze that would bewilder ours. For instance, here's this of Lundy—what are we to do with him? He hath deserved death, and cheaply; but I for one am not desirous to begin our rule by an execution. What say you?'

'Hew him in pieces before the Lord, like Agag,' said Mr. Hewson.

Sure, if ever a face said, 'Who hath asked for your opinion?' 'twas the face of Mr. George Walker, as he turned it upon this intruder. And scarce was its expression more friendly when he looked at Adam Murray, who, contrary to all the rules of manners, had opened the

debate without being asked.   He gave a ' Hem '
that was meant to introduce a speech from the
chair ; but 'twas altogether fruitless, they were
already too far aloft to heed his lure ; and that
which he would fain have constituted into a
council-meeting was degenerated into a mere
party of friends consulting at their ease and
leisure.

One after another, the gentlemen assembled
stated their views ; and upon the whole, each
desired to spare Lundy's life—not so much
because they wished to show mercy upon him
as for the reason Adam had stated, that 'twas
an ill fashion of opening their rule by blood-
shed.   Mr. Hewson, no whit abashed, had a
reason to render back to each one, why he
judged amiss, and why Lundy should suffer
the due punishment of his treason.   But Mr.
Walker, a little offended at their lack of ob-
servance towards him, never opened his lips
until they had all said their say.   From time to
time I cast mine eyes upon him, each time
with a new motion of wonder how a grown
man should show himself so childish.

At last it began verily to seem as though
they should be brow-beat into hanging Lundy
against their will, so full was Mr. Hewson of
his instances, and so instant with his reasons.

'The man,' said he, with a gesture that

seemed designed to clinch the matter, 'hath
been delivered into your hands, and it will be
at your peril—ay, and you shall dearly answer
it—if you suffer him to escape!'

At that Mr. Walker spoke, and spoke with
great simplicity, so that this time I wondered
how a man that had just shown himself so
childish should show himself now so worshipful.

'I think, sir, under your favour,' said he to
Mr. Hewson, 'that you're mistaken; and 'tis
just because he is so entirely delivered into our
hands that I would give my voice for letting
him go. Your instances are something anti-
quated; and mercy to our enemies hath been
taught us since then.'

'This man,' said Mr. Hewson, as ready to
hold his own with Mr. Walker as with any of
the rest, 'is not our enemy alone, but the enemy
of God as well.'

'You say truth,' said Mr. Walker; 'and so I
think I'd be for leaving him in God's hands for
punishment.' He spoke reverently, far more
so than Mr. Hewson. 'We have suffered—or
been in danger of suffering—so much from his
treason, that I should fear lest something of
revenge for our own injuries should mingle with
our zeal, and defile it.'

''Tis a scruple very honourable to your cloth,
sir,' said Adam, with respectful countenance,

whereat Mr. Hewson took his turn to look slighted.

'Let him but show his face in the street,' said he, 'and that question will be settled without either trial or judge. Did you chance to pass by his house last night, may I ask? and did you see the men he had so nearly betrayed standing around it ten or a dozen deep, lest he should escape?'

'I did,' said Adam gravely; 'and I agree with you, sir, that had he shown himself, he'd have been torn in pieces. That, beyond question, had been a great misfortune; for it could not have failed to damage the cause.'

'The cause, sir, give me leave to tell you,' said Mr. Hewson, 'is too good to take damage from an act of justice.'

'Nay, sir,' said Mr. Walker—and again he spoke with gravity and simplicity—'there is no cause so good that it will bear to be handled with bloody hands.'

Never a man put me in so many minds as this Mr. Walker, what to think of him. When he was pompous and arrogant, I contemned him; when he was martial—and truly he was as good a soldier as any man among those that had been bred to it, and so they said themselves—I marvelled at his cloth; but when, as at this time, the real goodness of the man broke through the outer husks of manner and littleness, I could not choose but reverence him; and I understood the motives of Adam and Major Baker in recommending him to be joint-Governor of the town.

That it was the work of these two came out in the course of the talk that we all fell into, leaving the question of Lundy's fate still undetermined. I was so unmannerly as to put the question, why Adam himself had not been named our Governor? seeing that he and he only had been able, the day before, to make himself obeyed. Major Baker made haste to express his concurrence with me.

'Madam,' said he, 'give me leave to assure you that it's his own fault and no one else's. The office was offered to him; and there's not a man of us but would have been happy to serve under him, and done it loyally, too. But he could not be brought to accept; I own I'm at a loss to understand his objections.'

'Why, truly,' said Adam, 'I can but marvel at that, for I stated them plainly enough at the council. 'Tis a wise man that knows his own gifts—and that wise man am I! In the field, now—there I know what to do, and I make no secret that I'd rather lead than follow. But in matters of policy—no! There I'm as simple as a child, and, happily for you all, I know it.'

He ended with his great, good-humoured laugh, and turning to my father, he appealed to him.

'Have I given proof of my wisdom herein, uncle,' said he, 'or have I not?'

'I cannot tell,' said Mr. Murray; 'for I, too, should have said you were a man very fit for the office.'

'I thought you had known me better,' said Adam sedately. 'What use am I in a formal council-meeting, for instance? None. Here 'tis different; I can say what I think, because there's no need for speech-making or graces of diction. But in public! why, I am but a dumb dog, and you all know it. You want one that can bark.' And he made a gesture towards Mr. Walker.

Now, I have often heard that gentleman censured for his jealousy; but when I remember how he broke out in reply to this speech of Adam's, I scarce can believe him guilty of any such thing.

'Sir,' said he, 'you are mistaken; you are utterly and entirely mistaken, both in your estimate of your own powers and of ours. When I remember you yesterday, first in the street and afterwards at the council-board, faith, sir, there was none of us, not one, spoke half so easily, or half so much to the point.'

'It's an easy matter,' said Adam, 'to speak out that which hath been boiling in one's heart for months, especially when a man hath no reason to care whether he keeps within bounds of courtesy or not. You were all too tender of Lundy, his feelings and his prejudices. Why, the man hath *no* feelings that can be wounded; and even now, could you see into his soul, you'd find he is but grieved at being hindered from perfecting his treason, and mortified at losing the reward of it—no doubt he had it specified to him in black and white : such and such a dignity, and so much in cash. That he is unmasked, and hath lost the good opinion of many that were his friends, sure it troubles him not a whit; I'll warrant him!'

'There were some upon the walls to-day, said Major Baker, 'would have given much to know what offers were being made to yourself, when you and my Lords Strabane and Abercorn walked to and fro so long, and plunged so deep in talk.'

'They're welcome to hear it for me,' said Adam. 'A commission of Colonel of Horse in King James's army, and a thousand pound in gold—that was what they offered me if I would perfect the Articles that Lundy had begun. I told them 'twas a poor kind of compliment to try to buy me for so little!'

He rose, and was leaving us, with a careless shaking of the garments, as who should say, 'Enough of so profitless a subject!' but our curiosity would not endure to be so thwarted.

'Tell us, I pray you, Adam,' said Rosa, 'what you said to Lundy.'

'I did but tell him to his face, cousin,' said he, 'what all these gentlemen were thinking— that he was either a knave, and not to be trusted, or else a fool, and incapable to bear rule. And as he seemed to question my judgment, I gave him the history of the whole campaign, from point to point, showing him why, though we were usually victorious in the particulars, we were beaten upon the whole. 'Twas wholesome hearing for him ; or would have been, had it come a little sooner.'

''Twas wholesome hearing for all of us,' said Mr. Walker warmly, as Adam quitted the room, 'and very humbling, to be shown how easily and how completely he had hoodwinked us all by his cunning. When he handled the case of Dungannon, I knew not whom to be most wroth at—Lundy, for having laid the trap, or George Walker, for having gone into it so foolishly.'

'I admired the most,' said Wamphray, 'when he came to handle the Articles that were on the table. Lundy's change of front,' said he to Rosa and me, 'when he found that his attempt to browbeat Adam had merely landed him in a thorough exposure, was as complete as sudden. He did all but admit the truth of everything Adam had charged him with. "But," said he, " now that things are come to such a pass, sure, the only course for us is to capitulate on the best terms we can procure;" and fell to showing him why he should set his hand to the paper, like the rest. But Adam looks deliberately round upon the councillors, as counting them, which I believe he was doing. "Sir," says he, "you know as well as I do that articles of this kind are not valid save when agreed to in a full council of war, which this," quoth he, " is not, for half your officers are not in it, nor near it. No, sir," he continues; " the true council of war to-day is in the streets, and thither I'll go to consult;" and so went away and left them by the ears together over the order in council that sent away the English troops, which Lundy had drawn up in concert with their officers. 'Twas as unexpected as shocking to the most of those that were in session with him at that moment when Mr. Mogredge, encouraged by Adam's plain speaking, took heart of grace and produced it.'

Here, then, we had the history of our little
revolution, which, sure, was no less important
to us than the great one to the entire kingdom.
But we were yet to be witnesses of a sequel to
it that matched, upon our small scale, one of
the features of that greater one.

For Rosa and I, having been to Thomas
Ash's home to ask for his child that had been
sick, were returning at dusk.   One day of good
government had made so great a difference in the
state of the streets, that it was a pure pleasure
to consider it.   The day before, when I went
abroad on the same errand, I had been delayed
for hours before it was possible to make my
way home again.   This evening anyone, the
timidest, might have gone from end to end of
the town without cause to tremble.   It was
scarce to be credited that the mere sense of
security should have wrought so great a
change.

My father met us on the threshold, and there
we stood speaking together, when we saw,
coming out of Mr. Walker's house, a little
further down the street, a common soldier
bearing a great load of match on his back.
Bent and burdened as he went, there was
something familiar in the gait of this soldier.
He looked to right and left of him as he came

out of the house, as if debating which way it were best to go. From the wall at the end of the streets there came the sound of a sentry's challenge; 'twas the hour of the changing of the watch. That settled the soldier's mind; and I think his hesitation, as well as the decision he came to, settled ours. We knew him; it was no other than Colonel Lundy.

Having chosen to go by the Diamond, he was obliged to pass us, and that very near. Had we had time to think of it, I make no doubt we had turned our eyes away from him, for who would choose to exult over a fallen enemy? and he, had he taken thought, had sure done anything rather than encounter recognition. But so it fell out, that in passing us he looked up; our eyes met, and he saw himself known.

'You would not betray me?' said he, in a low voice. Ay, and it trembled upon the words, for all he is a soldier.

'Go in peace for me,' replied my father, as softly.

So he passed out of our sight, round the corner of the Diamond, and we saw him no more. And that was the last of Colonel Lundy in Derry, for by means of his disguise and a pass from Mr. Walker he got clear away.

'See the reward of treachery!' said my father to us, as we came into the house.

'And what is that, sir, I pray you?' asked Mr. Hewson, looking up from his papers.

'One flying in disguise, in contempt and peril, that might have kept the most honoured place among us, as he held it,' said Mr. Murray sadly.

'What?' said Mr. Hewson, springing to his feet. 'Is he got away? I will go out and raise the people. I will——'

'You will, I hope, refrain from making mischief which you will find it hard to mend!' said my father sharply.

His eyes sparkled; 'tis easy at times to see that he hath been a passionate man in his youth.

'Mischief, sir!' said the other, as angrily as he. 'It is not I that will have caused it, but those that wink at evil-doing.'

And so went forth at the top of his speed, but returned after half an hour a little crestfallen. Rosa desired to know from him, partly, I believe, to cheer him, what had happened.

'Moderate your curiosity, young mistress,' said he angrily. 'Will talking of that which hath been ill done mend it?'

'But this, sure,' I said, 'scarce stands in need of mending.'

'Mending!' said he, for the man, I believe, was half beside himself with anger. 'Ay, truly, it stands in need of mending, and of marring to boot, before 'tis ready for mending. The enemies of the Lord have it their own way at this time. Will it be for ever, think you? No, verily! Will the Lord suffer such to triumph, think you, as have no mind to walk in His ways? He hath cast down those that feared Him *least* from their high seats. Was it, think you, merely to set up those that fear Him *little* in their stead?'

Rosa looked at him more than half frighted at his vehemence; I, with indignation at his violence and intolerance.

''Tis a riddle, sir, I perceive, that you would set us,' I replied to his question. 'I protest I am not in the spirits to care for such diversions.' Then, as he frowned upon me, I took Rosa by the hand. 'Come away, dear,' I said to her. 'We, like Mr. Hewson himself, for the matter of that, shall know the answer when it comes.'

And so, making him a deep curtsey, I turned upon my heel and left him.

Strange, that the next news of Lundy should be of the surrender of Culmore to the enemy,

which he by his falsehoods had procured on his
way to the ships that had waited for him at
Greencastle.   And stranger yet, to me, that
Mr. Hewson, for all his airs of prophecy, never
claimed it as proof of his wisdom, but left each
of us to draw the conclusion that liked him.

END OF VOL. II.

BILLING AND SONS, PRINTERS, GUILDFORD.